MANHUNT:
THE NIGHT STALKER

MANHUNT: THE NIGHT STALKER

HOW I BROUGHT SERIAL PREDATOR DELROY GRANT TO JUSTICE

COLIN SUTTON

JB

First published in the UK by John Blake Publishing
an imprint of Bonnier Books UK
Fourth Floor, Victoria House, Bloomsbury Square,
London WC1B 4DA
Owned by Bonnier Books
Sveavägen 56, Stockholm, Sweden

www.facebook.com/johnblakebooks ◉
twitter.com/jblakebooks ◉

First published in paperback in 2021

Paperback: 978-1-78946-225-8
eBook: 978-1-78946-420-7
Audio: 978-1-78946-254-8

British Library Cataloguing-in-Publication Data:

A catalogue record for this book is available from the British Library.

Design by www.envydesign.co.uk

Printed and bound in Great Britain by Clays Ltd, Elcograf S.p.A.

3 5 7 9 10 8 6 4 2

John Blake Publishing is an imprint of Bonnier Books UK
www.bonnierbooks.co.uk

AUTHOR'S NOTE

I will not use the true name for any of the victims in this account; although almost all have now passed on I believe that to respect their memories I should maintain their anonymity.

CONTENTS

PROLOGUE

Delroy Grant – dubbed the Night Stalker – was one of the nation's most wanted men, a shocking sex predator. During his seventeen-year reign of fear, he established a clear MO. Target an elderly woman, living alone. Visit them at night. Remove a window pane and slide in. Unscrew the lightbulbs. Cut the power at the electricity meter. Rip out the telephone wires. Tiptoe to the bedroom. Wake the victim by shining a torch in their eyes while ensuring their silence with a gloved hand across their mouth. What followed for his terrified victims was an unspeakable ordeal, often lasting hours heavy with the threat of sexual violence – even in the cases where he controlled himself.

His crimes had dreadful consequences – of which his victims spoke with courage and heart-rending simplicity:

'This has ruined the winter years of my mother's life,' said one victim's son.

'I don't have nightmares now, but I make sure I take certain measures. I have to leave a light on, I make sure all the doors and windows are locked, even in the summer. I cannot sleep if they are open because I think he will be able to get back in,' said another victim, aged 84.

'I cannot emphasise enough my feelings of embarrassment and humiliation during the attack and after. I feared for my life. I believed I was going to be murdered,' remembered one more victim, aged 88.

On a crisp, dry November night in 2009 the surveillance sergeant was controlling his team from the back of the convoy, not that anybody looking on would have realised it was a convoy. Or at least that was the plan, despite the fact that, unusually, one of the police cars had deliberately been piloted by an alert officer to a position in front of the target vehicle. He was remaining unseen but effectively slowing everything down so that those desperately trying to catch up behind had a better chance. They had closed in on the grey Vauxhall Zafira despite it being enthusiastically driven at more than 60 mph at times, except, of course, for when it passed the speed cameras. Its driver was far too smart to attract unnecessary attention that way.

The Zafira was now about three miles from the observation area, far enough away from where it had first been spotted for the driver not to connect the coming police request to stop with where he had been. And more importantly, with what he had been doing just fifteen minutes previously. If it turned out he was not the right man, then there was still a good chance that the huge observation going on in a vast swathe of south-east London would remain a secret. And that was vital to the operation, the one thing which the team simply could not risk was their surveillance leaking out.

As the Zafira signalled to turn into Witham Road, a residential street off Elmers End Road by Birkbeck railway station, it was time to move in. Following him unnoticed would be quite difficult in the maze of quiet side streets. And, if the driver was who they suspected – who they hoped – then he might even be seeking another target. After all, suburban streets at the dead of night? That was his hunting ground.

'Go, go, go, take him now,' spat the team leader into the covert microphone mounted on his sun-visor, the words causing his heart to race a little as they always did, no matter how many times he'd said them. Its highly trained driver responded instantly and the anonymous dark-green Ford Mondeo came alive, overtaking two carloads of colleagues and moving to within inches of its quarry. The wail of the siren and the flood of blue LEDs bullied the Zafira driver into braking sharply as he pulled to the kerb.

That driver was Delroy Grant, a 52-year-old Jamaican who had lived for almost all his life in England. He was no stranger to the police in his youth but had apparently kept out of trouble for almost twenty years. Nevertheless, he knew he had plenty to hide and so, albeit unconvincingly, he said his name was Kelvin Grant. 'But sorry, officers, I don't have any ID with me.'

The Zafira being registered to the Motability scheme was no help in instantly verifying his identity, so the officers began to search through the car. When, in the centre console, they found some bank cards in the name of Delroy Grant and his wife Jennifer, he knew that he had to tell the truth – that if he maintained the lie, he faced arrest anyway, on suspicion of stealing the cards. So he decided to come clean. But naturally, those who give false names to police often have something to hide; knowing the score he had probably imagined what was going to happen.

When the officers told him he was being arrested he reacted in a quietly compliant manner, despite knowing deep down that, at last, his game was very probably up. The clothing, crowbar and balaclava in the car, his strange attire with multiple layers on top and bottom, and the telling discovery of a small, powerful torch in his trouser pocket would see to that. At that point he would have had no idea that he had been tailed all the way from Shirley where, the officers had been told by their invisible colleagues, he had been trying to break into a bungalow.

All of which of course was really of incidental evidential consequence. He was intelligent enough to know that this was it, the day he had long feared but which he had always tried his utmost to postpone, had arrived. He had had a good run, only one close-call in seventeen years, but once he gave his DNA that would be it. A cotton wool bud dragged across his cheek through his gaping mouth by a rubber-gloved hand. That was all that would be needed to prove that his time was up: that he was indeed the Night Stalker.

Chapter 1

'CAN YOU JUST TAKE A LOOK?'

There is an old joke in the police that if you go away on holiday you might find yourself transferred when you get back. It was not quite as stark as that, but three absences I had in 2009 resulted in some quite momentous changes in my professional life – and might ultimately have affected when and even if the Night Stalker were to be captured.

First, I took a day off when our new superintendent came to visit my team at Barnes. On my return I was told that my latest boss was not impressed with the way I had 'decorated' my desks and surroundings in the office. The room was open-plan and I shared a space at the end of the long office at Jubilee House, Putney, with my detective inspectors. The team had christened it 'The Executive Lounge' and erected notices to that effect.

I had four desks, or tables, and in an effort to personalise my space, in common with many who have their own workspace, there were the photographs of my children. But there were also some unusual mementos: a small Scalextric-type circuit with two racing Minis and a micro-sized dartboard, both of which

1

had been birthday gifts from my children, and in pride of place, hanging from the ceiling above me, a plastic flying pig, battery-operated, which would fly around in tethered circles when switched on. This I occasionally used during meetings to emphasise my view that what I was being told really would not happen.

Evidently the Superintendent had felt these were unbefitting of a senior investigating officer (SIO); maybe that was correct but I could not help thinking that the objections should have been raised with me personally rather than vicariously through my junior officers. Whether this really quite minor irritation initiated a question mark against me and my team I shall never know, but what happened a few weeks later that Easter left me in no doubt that we were firmly in somebody's sights.

We had been on call, a status that lasted from 7 am Tuesday to 7 am the following Tuesday. It meant that we had a long weekend off to follow, although as it was Easter weekend, we would in any case have been on leave Friday to Monday. During the week we had dealt with the initial response to nine murders, handing eight over to other investigation teams but for the other retaining responsibility for the investigation ourselves. It had gone well – my team by then was just so experienced and skilful that it was more than a match for any criminal. They solved the case quickly, charging the murderer within forty-eight hours of the call.

It had been a busy week, long hours and with little rest, juggling the need to respond at the scenes of new suspicious deaths with the flurry of activity involved in the first days of a murder investigation. By Thursday afternoon there were whispered suggestions throughout the office that a visit to the pub after work would be in order. I would usually always tag along for a bit, feeling really it was part of my role as leader, but on this occasion I had too much to do at home. Appreciating though that it was just what the team needed, I announced at about 3 pm that they should go. It was not much of a concession – almost all of them were due to finish at 4 pm anyway – but it was the least they deserved after their sterling efforts of the past seven days. So, while the greater part of the team adjourned to the Jolly Gardeners, I drove down the A3, beating the rush-hour traffic to arrive home around 4 pm.

Within half an hour I was called by DI Sarah Rees. She had been at court and so had not gone to the pub; arriving back at the office she had found the place deserted except for the Superintendent. She told me that she was being asked where everyone was. I said I would speak to the boss and explain. She made him the offer but, astoundingly, he was unwilling to talk to me. I told Sarah to relay that they were probably all at the pub, that they deserved it after their Herculean efforts during the week from hell – and that to thank them personally, perhaps the solution would be to join them and get a round in.

At 8 pm Sarah called me again. The Superintendent had been with her at the office for a full three hours, making her go through in some detail the current situation of all our outstanding investigations, our budgets, etc. – everything that was ultimately my responsibility and which I would have expected my supervisor to have wanted to pick over with me. Sarah added that she got the impression 'there was an agenda'. She was a relatively new addition to my team and I didn't know how much faith to place in her judgement; nevertheless, I considered my cards well and truly marked.

My relationship with the Superintendent was, thereafter, pretty frosty. This didn't stop my team being turned to when a quick and decisive result was required for a high-profile gang murder well off our patch in east London; a black teenager stabbed to death at a time when gang violence in the capital was a really hot potato. We delivered it for him, very quickly, thanks in most part to some stunning witness-handling work by two of my most experienced detective sergeants. Nevertheless, I was under no illusion that this choice was pragmatic rather than a signal of improved regard. I carried on doing my job to the best of my ability as usual but official meetings and even social occasions where I had to be in the company of my immediate manager became things for me to dread.

In early April 2009 I went on holiday for a week. It had been booked for some time and therefore couldn't be rearranged to enable me to meet the recently installed boss of London Homicide, Chief Superintendent Hamish Campbell, when he came for a 'review the fleet' meeting on taking over the Command – not that he would have expected me to drop everything for that. On my return I found a pleasant email from him, explaining how he had enjoyed his visit, how he found the team to be in good spirits and well-motivated and that he would like me to come and see him so he and I could meet properly. It was in stark contrast to the check-up visit from the Superintendent at Easter and accurately reflected their very different leadership styles. I made a quick call to his PA and I was booked in for a morning meeting at Scotland Yard a couple of days later.

Hamish Campbell was a very experienced investigator,

perhaps best known by colleagues and the public as the SIO who led the Jill Dando murder investigation. Tall, balding, well-groomed and well-spoken, he welcomed me with a cup of coffee and began chatting, generally, about the murder command, outstanding cases and – inevitably – my team's success with serial killer Levi Bellfield. The whole meeting seemed nothing out of the ordinary really, a predictable and friendly catch-up. But then came a question I had not expected.

'What do you know about Operation Minstead?'

'I know that it has been going a long time, a long series of rapes of the elderly in their homes. I know Simon Morgan is the SIO and that there is DNA – that's about it.'

That basic idea of the operation was, I am sure, a pretty common one among those who were not involved in it. It is interesting to me now, looking back, that the general understanding focussed on the rapes; it would only be much later when I read the whole sad story that I was to realise Minstead (as usual, a place name chosen from the *Gazetteer of Great Britain* – in this case, a small village near Lyndhurst in the New Forest) was a great deal more complicated than that.

'Yes. It is something about which the Commissioner is deeply concerned. He has suggested to me that it ought to be a priority for the Command and I thought that, given you have a recent record of success in a high-profile case involving a serial sex offender, you might be able to use your investigative acumen to bring something to the table.'

'And when the Commissioner suggests…'

There was no need for me to finish the sentence, the smile it drew from my boss showed that he understood it as much as I did.

I hesitated. While it was reassuring to be spoken of in those terms by the new chief superintendent, I was not clear exactly what he might be suggesting. With a degree of naivety I asked, 'Do you mean my team taking it on as our investigation, or just for me to do a review of what they've got?'

'No, a review, definitely just a review. By you alone, an investigative review to see if there are any opportunities to catch him that might have been missed.'

'But surely, I know it has been reviewed lots of times – indeed, did I not see that the Serious Crime Review Group had just recently embarked upon another one?'

'Yes, they did . But I don't mean the sort of administrative review that checks every dot and comma in the HOLMES [Home Office Large Major Enquiry System] account, that's not what I need to know, not what we need to find out. I want you to cut through all the extraneous stuff and look at the investigation. The leads, the intelligence, the possible lines of enquiry. A fresh set of eyes, you know.'

That sort of review – one with a practical purpose far beyond housekeeping – appealed to me. I thought for a moment how Hamish must have done his homework, that he knew what made me tick. He had captured my interest almost immediately and closed the deal as he went on:

'Some of them have been so close to it for so long there just might be something they're missing. You've got plenty of initiative, you can be a little creative. Can you just take a look?'

My initial reaction was that there was nothing for me to lose in taking, as he put it, 'a look'. So I agreed there and then, suggesting that I would do some research into the crimes and the investigation for a few days before he announced to the

Minstead team that I would be coming. We both knew, though it went unsaid, that I probably would not be all that welcome – SIOs are notoriously protective of their own operations and all the more so when it is one to which they have dedicated years of their career. Who, in any profession, would relish the idea of a peer picking over every last detail of their as yet unsuccessful work?

I went back to the office at Putney where I asked Clive Grace, now my intelligence DS, to print me out a few things to be getting on with and then just tried to keep working as normal. I was in part excited at the prospect of getting to grips with such a difficult and important investigation and yet in part terrified that I would fail and, in some ways blemish the record and reputation I had worked so hard to earn in the Levi Bellfield cases.

That investigation, over three long years and culminating in a five-month trial, had sent that most predatory and infamous of serial murderers to prison forever, three times over, for the murders of Marsha McDonnell, Amélie Delagrange and Milly Dowler. I knew I would forever be remembered as the detective who had led the team that put him away but even that great success had not completely eradicated my self-doubt. I was 48 years old, two years away from the end of a police career in which many would argue I had achieved great things yet still, faced with a difficult and very public challenge, my initial reaction was that I might not be up to it. The other striking feeling I had was more sadness than fear – I knew in my heart this would be the final case on my workload, the last team I would lead.

This time round though I found it much easier to deal with

7

and rationalise. After all, it was really an assignment with no personal risk to me. All I had to do was have a look through the papers, talk to the team and then see if I could suggest anything to help. If I found something useful, all well and good. If I came up with nothing there would be no shame for me. The case had confounded a number of highly skilled and experienced senior investigators over many years. Hadn't it?

It is very unusual, unknown even, for any gossip relating to staff moves or responsibilities to remain a secret for long in the Metropolitan Police. There are just too many people involved in the planning, the news leaks effortlessly out and, at every level, other people's careers seem always to be a topic of conversation. It was therefore no surprise to me, just a few days later, when DC Gary Cunningham sidled up to me in the Boat House pub next door after work and asked if the rumours were true.

'What rumours would they be then, Gary?'

'That you are leaving us to take over as SIO on Minstead?'

I didn't want to lie to him and also, as he was one of the very best officers out of the excellent team I had, it had occurred to me that he might be willing to come across and help me, so I replied with a pretty straight bat. 'I have been asked to go and take a look, do a sort of review to see if there might be another way of solving it. You never know, I might well need some help from somebody I trust.'

Gary was much more direct in his reply.

'No way I'd want to be involved in that poisoned chalice. They're doing you up like a kipper, boss. Getting rid of you, smashing up the team. But not only that, they got you moved over to the biggest crock of shit in existence. You've got no chance of succeeding. I told you after the trial [nobody ever needed to say the Bellfield trial, it was always just 'the trial'] it was a shame you couldn't retire then.'

I smiled at his analysis, which for all I knew might have been spot on, but I had already realised that a desire was still burning in me.

'Don't write me off yet, Gary. It's a shame we can't all do it together as a team again, but I think I'm a bit like George Foreman or Joe Bugner. An ageing heavyweight who everyone thinks is past it. But I'm pretty sure I've still got one more fight left in me.'

And in my own mind I was certain that fight was about to begin.

Chapter 2

THE FIRST VISIT

I was born, and indeed grew up in, north London, and my police career had taken me to work first all across the capital to the north of the river and then later to the south-west. There was though a quarter of the city that had remained virtually unknown to me. The south-east part, from the Thames south, round anti-clockwise to the A23 – which just happened to be the exact area in which all the Minstead offences had taken place.

I saw that as a positive – aside from the ninety-mile round trip – braving the M25 each day from my home in Surrey, for which I was promised the use of a police car that never actually materialised. Police officers being somewhat parochial, many tended to remain in roughly the same part of London throughout their careers. I knew the chances were that I would know nobody there, other than by sight or nodding acquaintance, so there should be no awkwardness in my having to pronounce on the work of friends. I was, though, all too aware that, among the rest of us, the reputation of the detectives in that part of London had over the years become somewhat tarnished. Rachel Nickell, Stephen Lawrence, Daniel Morgan and Damilola Taylor were the high-profile investigations that, one way or another, had added fuel to that particular fire; the rest of the Met spoke loosely of nepotism, incompetence and even the suggestion of corruption in the Met's south-east divisions. Whether this notoriety was justified or simply the result of unfounded rumour it was real, and it meant I resolved to keep my wits firmly about me. I had no illusions that what I was about to embark upon would be easy, either professionally or personally. Nor, I thought, could I take cooperation from my colleagues there for granted. I was going to have to have a steel and resolve in my dealings with them, which was never normally the way I liked to do things.

I made a call before my first visit, to the lone detective inspector on the Minstead Operation, Nathan Eason, a man I had never met. I learned that he had not long been promoted and posted to the Homicide and Serious Crime Command, that he hadn't chosen to go to Minstead (in truth, I was to discover, very few had), but our conversation was upbeat and I warmed to him even over the phone. This initial impression was thankfully absolutely correct – he turned out to be an extremely capable, realistic and supportive lieutenant for me over the coming months. He said that he welcomed someone else coming to take a look, that he was not convinced they were on the right track but felt that he did not have the authority or the length of service on the Minstead team to make radical suggestions. I understood his position entirely. I found both his attitude and his manner immensely encouraging. One thing he said did though make me do a double take:

'I'll see if I can get Mr Morgan to come in so you can see him.'

I was taken aback by this. Naturally I had assumed the senior investigating officer would have been there, working on his only live investigation, for most of the time.

'Is he busy elsewhere then?'

'No, it's just that he is so unwell with his back and his drugs that he works mostly from home.'

This surprised me but also awakened a distant memory. I was vaguely aware that Superintendent Morgan had endured long periods of sick absence, but I had not realised that he had ongoing issues. I was to find out that he had been involved in an awful assault, on duty, which had damaged his spine, and despite a number of lengthy and painful surgical interventions over many months he was still in considerable pain and had significant mobility issues.

It was the beginning of May 2009 when I made my first visit to Lewisham. Driving north up Lewisham High Street from Catford I looked at my surroundings while crawling in its ever-present traffic queue and realised that I was in a very different environment to that I had enjoyed in Putney and Barnes. The type of shops, the dress of pedestrians and the age of the cars were all clear pointers that the area was far, far less affluent. When I came across the police station, I was though slightly awed. A huge modern building of light brickwork with concrete trim, it was arranged in two wings connected by a glass flyover walkway above imposing iron gates, with a multi-storey car park at the rear. Built under the private finance initiative scheme by investment funds and with an ongoing cost to the Met of nearly £20 million per year, it was home in its larger, southern, wing to the Borough police, with their response, neighbourhood and detective teams as well as a large custody suite. In addition to Minstead, the smaller wing to the north housed four murder teams, some child protection officers and a detachment of mounted officers, with their immaculate stables to the rear. In time, walking past these each morning was guaranteed to cheer me up – even if I did not get to see any of the magnificent creatures being groomed, I could still inhale a deep breath of the sweet smell of haylage, reminding me instantly of the enjoyment I had had keeping horses years before. In the past I had found how the stresses of the day could be relieved by stopping off on the way home to put in a feed and just have a quiet chat with our horses. I wondered if, when Minstead got too much, I could repeat the trick with these huge but gentle animals stabled next door to my office.

As is often the case with modern city traffic management, there was a knack to approaching the station by car; if the obvious approach were used, then one-way systems and no entry signs meant a fiddly detour to make it to the vehicular entrance in Myron Place. I cursed myself for not working it out on a map before my first visit but eventually found the gate; a swipe of my warrant card at the barrier secured access and a friendly uniformed officer in the car park pointed my way to the murder squad offices. There, a passing DC told me Minstead was on the first floor and I wandered along until I found a man in an office, on his hands and knees on the floor, sellotaping A4 sheets of paper accurately together to form a large chart.

'You must be the analyst,' I said. He smiled back and introduced himself as Richard Moore, the Senior Analyst for the murder teams and the analyst dedicated to the Minstead team. I told him who I was and he took me along to the Minstead team room. It was quite large, the desks outnumbering the visible staff considerably. Within it were two partitioned, windowless offices and in one of those I found DI Nathan Eason. A tall, sturdy man standing at a desk with its surface more than four feet off the ground; it was the first time I had encountered one of these special adjustable units.

He extended his hand towards me.

'Excuse the desk. How is your back? You don't have to have spinal issues to be a senior officer on this investigation but it helps.'

Both in our earlier call and now in person I could tell this was a friendly man with a sense of humour and no apparent issue with my intrusion. We made the tortuous trip up flights of stairs, through swipe-access doors past murder-team offices and across the flyover to the canteen, where we sat at a table together over a cup of coffee.

I had my ubiquitous red A4 notebook in which I had listed the sorts of things I wanted to know about – the staffing levels, the policies for DNA elimination, the current workload, active lines of enquiry. These were all the basic things I would need to get a grip on, quickly, before looking at what exactly had been done. While I was surreptitiously ticking these off there really was no need. Nathan had enough common sense to know what I would be interested in and had obviously himself, at least mentally, prepared a similar list. So on top of his brief was he that he did most of the talking, running me through the current situation for about half an hour without the need for me to prompt or probe on more than a couple of occasions.

What he told me held a few surprises that moved me away

15

from some preconceptions I had around the Minstead case. First, the operational strength of the team was about eleven constables, augmented by three retired officers re-engaged as civilian investigators. He was the lone DI and there were three sergeants. With creditable if dispiriting frankness he described his view of half the team as 'the lame and lazy', a further quarter as not wanting to be there and a final quarter who were really committed to the case. He put himself in the final group, admitting that while he would not have chosen the posting he was there and determined to do his very best. I felt from the start that in whatever direction my review went he would be supportive and that we could work together.

He then explained that the rate of offending had increased in the previous few months and ran me through the policies in place that dictated the team's response to them – basically that they treated each offence as if it were a homicide, with full forensic examination of the scene, house-to-house enquiries, CCTV trawl and so on. I noted in my book how hard that must be with, effectively, a half-strength team and remarked so to Nathan. He shrugged and said that, yes, it was. Especially when there had been multiple offences on the same night.

Apart from responding to new offences, the main activity of the team was to obtain DNA elimination samples from a list of possible suspects. I had been aware that this was a line of enquiry (and had deep reservations about it, in any investigation, which I shall come to later), but hadn't realised that it was effectively the only line being taken day-to-day by the team – when not responding to new offences. I had some experience of the difficulties involved in a mass-screening DNA exercise from the small part I played in the investigation of the so-called

M25 rapist Antoni Imiela. The likelihood of success of such a screening is very dependent upon the accuracy and robustness of the criteria used to rule people in as potential suspects. I needed to know how the suspect pool had been devised and so asked Nathan what the criteria for inclusion on the list for elimination were.

He smiled. 'That's far too difficult for me to explain, essentially they come from Mr Morgan and they do change. You really need to speak to him about that.'

Which was in many ways our cue to adjourn back across the bridge and for me to meet Simon Morgan.

Nathan took me along the corridor past the Minstead room to Morgan's office where he bid me goodbye. Obviously, he thought it better for our first meeting to be in private. The door to the office was half-open so I knocked politely and peeped around it. I saw an empty chair with a desk in front of it, my attention grabbed by one end of it which was covered in around a dozen different pots and packages of assorted prescription drugs. For a moment I thought the Superintendent must have popped out, then I became aware of movement in the office near the floor. I looked down and saw that he was in fact still there but was doing some sort of stretching exercise, lying on his back and twisting. It reminded me of the routine the rather eccentric Australian fast-bowler Merv Hughes used to go through in the outfield to limber up before coming on for a new spell. I was a little taken aback, embarrassed in truth. His eyes met mine and I softly said, 'I can come back if it isn't convenient, sir.'

'No, don't worry, I gotta do this every now and then to ease my back. Come in.'

As Simon stood up and shook hands I was filled with horror. Soldiering on is one thing but he looked like a man in great distress. He moved slowly and jerkily, striving always to keep his back straight. His eyes seemed so sad and it appeared even speech was painful. I thought he really shouldn't have been at work but, I instantly concluded, he must be so dedicated, so caught up in his decade-long search for the Night Stalker that he couldn't bring himself to let go. I was at the same time sympathetic, admiring and appalled, feeling really guilty that my arrival to pick over his investigation was yet another source of stress and discomfort that he obviously could have done without. Pretty soon though, processing this very unfamiliar situation, I realised that my sense of real sympathy for this fellow human and detective had to be laid to one side if I were to properly do the job I had been given. Whatever his obvious personal difficulties I had to look at – and, ultimately judge – his investigation dispassionately and objectively if my review were to be of any use at all.

'Are we OK to have a chat through a few things now?' I asked.

'Well, we're having a supervisors' meeting tomorrow to review strategy, so it might be a good idea if you come along to that, see where we are and then we can speak afterwards.'

That seemed to make sense to me so I agreed, we spent a few minutes talking about where I should sit and how I should be introduced to the team (which was very much focussed on my being a reviewer not an investigator), then Simon took me down to the office where I met a few of the HOLMES and intelligence staff. The enquiry officers, I was told, were out swabbing suspects.

So ended my first day on Minstead. I asked what time the

meeting was the next day and found it was to be 10.30 am – at Simon Morgan's house. Which obviously was very unusual but apparently a frequent practice. I agreed to meet the others at the office at 9.30 am and left to battle with the M25 again, thinking that I had really learned only a little which would help me complete my task but a considerable amount which told me that this was going to be very different from any other job I had ever taken on.

Chapter 3

IT'S ALL ABOUT THE DNA

Wednesday, 6 May 2009. I arrived at Lewisham just after 9 am and was somewhat surprised to see that there were very few officers in the incident room. Those that remained explained that, while most of the supervisors were going straight to Simon Morgan's house for the meeting, the troops were visiting Croydon Police Station where overnight two reports had come in of potential Minstead offences in Shirley. I wandered round to Nathan's office and found him standing at his desk.

'Two more last night?' I enquired, hoping to find out a little more.

'Well, possibly. Probably. It all depends on whether they meet the Minstead criteria…' he replied, rolling his eyes slightly.

'I suppose I'll have to get my head around those…'

'Yeah, well, good luck with that,' he said, taking a long sip from his cup.

I made a mental note to explore this further later as I felt both intrigued and slightly troubled by it, but for the moment

I wanted to try to prepare for whatever the meeting for which we were about to set off held in store. I asked Nathan what was going to be discussed.

He exhaled wearily and began. 'You know yesterday I said you'd have to speak to Mr Morgan about the DNA elimination criteria? Well, OK, I'll give it a go because it might help you understand the meeting better.'

He told me that the major topic of conversation would be the elimination criteria for DNA swabbing. He was able to predict this with confidence because, well, it always was.

Essentially, there was a large pool of potential suspects – more than 30,000 men, he said. These had made the list because they were black – as every single victim had described their assailant – lived in the area where the Night Stalker offended, and were within an age range that meant they were assumed neither too young nor too old to have committed the first and most recent offences. From these, certain priorities were set, based on intelligence gained from witness statements, evidence retrieved from crime scenes and also on theories advanced by police officers. It was the latter which, to me, appeared unusual and I probed Nathan on it.

He told me by way of example: when a victim had said that she heard a motorcycle start just after the suspect had left her, men in the pool who had a licence to ride motorcycles, or were known to use them, became a priority. In another crime, a burglary in 2004, the victim told them that the man who broke in and assaulted her had remarked that his mother had died four years previously, and also that she had been 'let down by the government'. This had prompted a difficult, lengthy and ultimately fruitless line of enquiry to identify black men in the area whose mothers had passed away in 2000. These did at least have a basis and as such were less controversial, Nathan suggested, than some of the officer-advanced theories. Such as when somebody – not even a member of the team – had noticed that a few offences had been committed in streets where cables for Sky TV had recently been installed. The theory went on to advance that this would provide an excellent opportunity for the Night Stalker to perform reconnaissance and select targets while unnoticed. Therefore, anybody who worked for Sky or its sub-contractors had duly been pushed to the top of the list.

Nathan assured me that such speculation would form a large part of the meeting, his manner in saying so showing he did not need to add that it was a process he found somewhat pointless and wasteful. He then said that the rest of it would probably be about the various 'cutting-edge' actions that were being farmed out to universities and laboratories, all with the aim of discovering whether it were possible to get any useful identification information from the unknown DNA profile we had linking the offences. 'But,' he concluded, 'don't hold your breath.'

This was the first occasion on which I thought that DNA elimination might be a rather laboured exercise with constantly shifting priorities – but I sensed it probably was not to be the last. I wondered how difficult it must be for the officers. Those suspects in the target pool having grown up as black men in London during the 1970s and 1980s would, I thought, probably have good reason to be suspicious of their treatment as young men at the hands of the Metropolitan Police; it was likely that the current generation of officers would be paying a price for the sins of their fathers. It would surely mean that quite a few of those men selected for swabbing would be mistrusting and not consent to giving a DNA sample, either because they believed it might be misused or because they had a simple principle not to assist the police at all. Since it had to be assumed that if the real Night Stalker were himself asked for a swab he would probably withhold consent, each refusal would pose a real problem for the SIO. Should each refusal lead inevitably to arrest? Of course, further research would be needed in each instance before such drastic action – but given the small team and the demands of responding to new offences, how quickly and thoroughly might that be done? All this simply confirmed my long-held belief that mass DNA screening is so fraught with difficulty and so thirsty for resources that it ought only to be considered a tactic of last resort. I needed to find out – was Operation Minstead that desperate?

It was when I asked Nathan Eason about the success rate of the swabbing operation that I began to have serious doubts.

'How many swabs do we try to get each week – and how many do we actually achieve?' I casually enquired.

'We try for as many as we can but often it is really hard. Like last week, we got one. Just one.'

Unprepared for the hopelessness my question had inspired, I probed further. 'And how many men are currently on the priority list?'

'Well, five thousand two hundred as of now but of course it might well change after the meeting today,' replied Nathan, trying hard to be neutral in his tone. Our gazes met and I sensed he was reading what was coming but I said it anyway.

'One a week, five thousand two hundred to be done – that's

easy even for my limited mathematical ability. At that rate it would take us a hundred years.'

'Yeah,' said Nathan, resignedly. 'I don't think we've got that long…'

*

We arrived at Simon Morgan's beautiful detached house around thirty minutes later, pulling through the double gates and joining the handful of plain Met cars already parked behind the long ivy-clad brick wall. Following Nathan through the front door I saw one of the team's long-serving detective sergeants was in the kitchen, chatting to a lady I assumed to be Mrs Morgan.

'I don't expect he is up to that sort of exertion in his condition,' I heard the officer say – and the burst of laughter that followed indicated that he was very much a friend of the family, comfortable in cracking a risqué joke.

Nathan led me round to the left, into a large sitting room where a dozen or so chairs of various descriptions had been carefully arranged around its edge. It felt a bit like entering a dentist's waiting room and to a degree I felt a sense of nervousness as I took my seat. Among the chairs was one that was raised on blocks, similar to those found in care homes, modified to aid rising for those with mobility issues. As the meeting convened and Simon Morgan took the high seat he looked very much like an ancient king, holding court from his throne.

In opening, Simon introduced me to the assembled supervisors and stressed that my task was a short one: to see if there might be any missed opportunity that might help to progress the case. While this was accurate, spelling it out in terms like this would, I thought, do little to smooth my entry into the team. If I were them I would have been thinking that this stranger was there simply to discover my mistakes. The other officers introduced themselves to me individually by name, rank and role, and I made an obvious effort to give each of them a smiling 'Hello' and repeat their name. I had wanted to write their details down to make certain that I would remember them but thought it might appear too officious and antagonistic, so I decided to keep my hands conspicuously away from my notebook and trust to my memory.

First on the agenda was swabbing. DS Dave Meade, the office manager, gave the statistics for the previous week and essentially confirmed the difficulties that Nathan had already outlined for me, albeit in a more neutral manner. Next, Simon Morgan gave an update on the various scientific lines of enquiry. He spoke first at length of the work of the University of Santiago. Their efforts were to try to establish probable physical characteristics of the Night Stalker from from traces of DNA that he had left at crime scenes. As Nathan had indicated back at Lewisham, Simon was keen to stress that their work was 'cutting edge'; he described it as such several times. It was certainly an advancement of science to which I was completely oblivious and while the concept fascinated me and the potential for it as a crime-fighting tool was exciting, I felt a strong degree of cynicism. I would have thought that if it were genuinely believed to be possible it would have been something that would have been more widely known in the investigative community. I had by this time conceded that, irrespective of the optics, I needed to make notes and so scribbled an action to find out about this work going on in Chile. (Quite foolishly as it turned out, as after a few days I established the Superintendent had been referring to the University of Santiago de Compostela in Spain, and that no work was being done for Minstead in South America.)

The latest communication from the boffins indicated a strong possibility that the DNA showed the offender would have a genetic condition known as 'Red Ibo', which meant that while a person's facial structures were like those of a black person, they would be light-skinned with red or auburn hair and freckles. This was then built upon when one of the many e-fits completed by victims was considered, as it did indeed show a light-skinned black man with freckles. I kept my thoughts to myself but scribbled them in my red book. There were around a dozen e-fits that had been compiled over the long course of the investigation and what was striking about them was how different they all seemed to be. That said, the freckled one was most unlike all the others and so might be considered a real outlier. In any case, I reasoned, if the suspect's appearance were so startlingly distinctive wouldn't many if not most of the victims have noticed it? And how many Red Ibos were there in the suspect pool – indeed, in London? Surely if this were accurate it would make the task much more simple, easy even?

I wanted to ask the question but, probably wisely, I kept my own counsel. How, I silently mused, might this be compatible with the previous, 2006 prediction made by scientists that the suspect was probably from Trinidad or the southern Lesser Antilles? This had resulted in a visit to Trinidad by five Minstead officers who were ridiculed in the press as 'The Frying Squad' when they were pictured sunning themselves by the pool. The fruitless trip was, I knew, a rather sore point among the team and it was best again to keep my thoughts to myself. An excellent decision in hindsight: this line of enquiry was one of the most troublesome for my predecessors to try to follow.

In order to build up a database large enough to make comparisons statistically relevant, the Minstead team had decided to ask around two hundred male and female Met Police employees whose heritage was from the Caribbean to volunteer a DNA sample. This was, they were assured, to be stored separately from the general DNA database and used for no other purpose than comparison with the Night Stalker's DNA to try to better to understand where he might be from. The hope was that this would enable scientists to discern from which island, or even settlement, he or his family hailed. All did not go to plan, however. In May 2004, the *Daily Mail* had published a story thus:

> *The hunt for Britain's most prolific serial sex attacker is being thwarted by political correctness in the police force, it emerged last night. Detectives had hoped to catch the so-called Night Stalker by pinpointing his Caribbean origins using revolutionary DNA analysis. For the method to work, they wanted to carry out voluntary tests on Scotland Yard staff who originate from the West Indies. Their aim was to compare their DNA and family history with the suspect's to identify which island, or even town, he comes from. Now in a major setback to their 12-year investigation, they have been banned from taking samples after a warning about race 'sensitivity' from the Black Police Association.*

The report went on to quote one of the fifty employees who had offered to provide a sample and give details of their family origins:

'We wanted to help and now we've been told that we can't. It's political correctness gone crazy. This would be unusually reliable because the volunteers were serving police officers with no reason to disguise their backgrounds. It is understood that detectives were particularly anxious for the samples to be given as soon as possible because the Night Stalker is known to favour summer attacks.'

The Met issued a statement which the *Daily Mail* also ran with some comment:

Following a meeting with the BPA executive, its Metropolitan branch complained that the procedure did not apply to white officers. Then, acting on legal advice, senior officers at the Yard decided they did not want to go ahead without BPA backing. So, when volunteers turned up to give DNA swabs, they were told they could not take part. One officer was quoted as saying: 'We were really keen to help. We are astonished that the Association intervened. We don't see this as offensive, sensitive or racist in any way.' Another, whose grandmother came to Britain from the Caribbean three generations ago, said: 'It was a unique opportunity for ordinary police officers to help bring the perpetrator of some seriously sick crimes to justice. If they had wanted to take samples from white officers, the DNA lab would already have those samples, no question.' The restriction on using the police officers' DNA caused 'extreme frustration' among detectives involved in the Night Stalker inquiry,' a senior source told the Daily Mail. *He added, 'We cannot believe anyone would try to impede the investigation in this way. It is not helpful and it does the Association's reputation no good whatsoever.' Chief Inspector Leroy Logan, who chaired the Met's BPA, denied it had instructed members not to cooperate, the paper added, and insisted that individuals were free to do so if they wished. He said, 'We didn't feel comfortable being seen as taking a lead on this. But we didn't make the decision to call it off. It was the powers that be who were calling the shots.'*

The remainder of the meeting was taken up with an airing of suggestions for modification of the swabbing criteria (although on this occasion ultimately none was made; from the way it was discussed I sensed how regularly they *might* have been), and then some administrative items regarding staffing and vehicles. As I looked back over my notes I realised that every one I had made somehow related to the DNA profile. This prompted me to write in the margin: 'It's all about the DNA' – a small cue to myself that was to become ever more relevant.

As the meeting broke up Simon Morgan came over to me with a stapled bundle of A4 paper.

'This is a printout of a PowerPoint which gives you a good idea of the history of the investigation,' he said, helpfully.

I started to flick through it, thanking him for providing such a useful document. I came across a page that had a copy of a piece from *The Sun*, bearing a small photograph of its author, Crime Editor Mike Sullivan. I had, since the Levi Bellfield case, become good friends with Mike, finding him in all regards a completely trustworthy journalist who was actively supportive of the police, even when his editor wanted a different line to be taken. When I saw his picture, showing him several years ago when he still had a full head of hair, I smiled.

'You wanna watch that snake,' urged Simon Morgan. 'He does nothing but carp on and undermine us. I don't trust him one little bit.'

I muttered a reply of, 'Oh, right,' trying not to betray that that was far from my experience of the man. But Simon went on, telling a story which I am sure was meant to demonstrate Sullivan's turpitude but which I'm afraid I actually found quite amusing…

'At a press conference he [Sullivan] and others kept referring to our suspect as the "Night Stalker". I hate that nickname, I think it causes more fear in the community so I asked them to stop using it. I suggested they should call him "Minstead Man". Sullivan stuck his hand up and asked if, instead, they could call him the "Old Dear Hunter".'

Chapter 4

GETTING UP TO SPEED – THE 1990s

I spent the next several days buried in my office, going through the presentation Simon Morgan had given me, looking at the statements and actions for the most recently reported crimes and generally doing my best to assimilate what was by any standard a huge amount of information. A process that is time-consuming but one in which, experience had taught me, there can be no shortcut. Although there was no real urgency for me, I took enough material home with me to make sure I could put a few hours in over the weekend too; by Monday morning I wanted to be pretty much up to speed. It was a dynamic investigation and information was coming to the surface each day, so I needed to have the grounding in order properly to judge how new facts should be assessed in the context of what had gone before. But it was not just about enabling me to carry out my task efficiently – I knew that if I could demonstrate to the team that I had my finger on the appropriate pulses they would take me much more seriously. I needed to squash any thought that I might be there just for a cursory look and, more importantly, to show that I was going to be able to see through any misleading waffle or spin they might be tempted to throw my way.

It was clear though that while a quick run-through a PowerPoint presentation was going to give me a flavour, I needed to have a much deeper appreciation of the investigation's history if I were to play any meaningful role. There was no other way – I had to read my way through the whole complicated and long-running story. It was yet another weekend 'off' surrendering to 'The Job'. With no access from home to the HOLMES account it was necessary to spend two long days in my little office at Lewisham, the door shut, and invisible to the world, ploughing my way through a litany of one man's horrific abuse of the elderly.

The attack that – at the time – we thought was the first in the Minstead series occurred in Shirley, south of Croydon, on a Monday evening, 12 October 1992. The 84-year-old spinster victim was attacked in her bed by a black man who was wearing a balaclava. He held her down, pinning her to her bed as she awoke to be confronted by a masked silhouette in the darkness, virtually blinded by the beam of his torch pointing directly into her eyes. He had broken in by a side kitchen window and, before stealing £25 cash, a pocket watch and jewellery, raped her. Unusually, he had kissed her, both on the cheek and mouth, during her ordeal, pulling her face to his with such force that he dislodged her dentures.

When the intruder had concluded his two-hour crime, the victim went to try to call for help; moving painfully through her small, tidy bungalow she found that he had removed many of the light bulbs from their sockets. With a show of defiant courage the Minstead victims seemed to possess in abundance, she found her small set of steps in the dark and replaced a bulb, giving her the light she needed to raise the alarm. Grabbing her telephone, she found it dead – the first of many helpless victims to find that the Night Stalker had cut the only lifeline they might have had to the outside world. She dressed quickly and went to her niece's house nearby, telling her she had been burgled. And, once the police were summoned, she confided in them that she had been raped.

Once the officers had arrived the process began. There is no escaping it: if a rape has taken place and is to be investigated, there is no option but to subject the victim – a person already at their lowest point having been physically and mentally debased – to an uncomfortable and undignified examination in the hope of securing evidence. While great progress has been made in making this procedure as supportive as possible, no matter how muted the wallpaper, how soft the furnishings nor how well-trained and empathetic the officers, ultimately it is always going to be unpleasant.

The swabs were taken and sealed and, together with her bedding and the pyjamas she had been wearing, sent to the Met Police Forensic Science Laboratory at Lambeth for examination. Both the victim's pyjama bottoms and the vaginal swabs tested positive for semen. At that time, it was not possible for the still-fledging DNA profiling techniques to extract a profile from the semen. While its presence corroborated the victim's story and indeed in many ways would prove the rape, as a means of identification it was useless. The investigation by the local divisional CID, led by a detective inspector, as were all rape cases, then stalled. There was no other evidence available to identify the attacker, local enquiries had proven fruitless. The likelihood was that the rapist would only face justice if, at some later date, he committed another similar offence where he was either careless or less fortunate and left the police some trace of his identity.

Although the list of offences I was reading through, in 2009, showed there were thirty-two further 'attacks during the following six years, these had been added to the list comparatively recently. They were offences reported at the time during the 1990s, when it was not realised that there was a serial offender on the loose – and so they were all treated as separate, one-off burglaries. It was not until the early hours of Saturday, 5 September 1998 that a further rape was committed, one which yielded a DNA profile matching that from the 1992 offence. Six years on, a series had emerged.

The 81-year-old lady lived alone in a bungalow in a quiet, narrow cul-de-sac in Warlingham, just over the border in the Surrey Police area. She had severe mobility issues, having had a double hip replacement, suffered from arthritis and was dependent on a stick to walk. The bungalow had been her home for eleven years, nearly ten of those alone since her husband had passed away. As answering the door to her home help or neighbours was difficult she had left a key to her rear patio doors on a string on the fence at the back. It was out of obvious sight but apparently readily found by the Night Stalker. There was no need to force entry here – he simply let himself in with the key.

The old lady had retired to bed at around eleven o'clock and was awoken some three or four hours later when she became aware of someone in her bedroom. She opened her eyes to the terrifying sight of a masked man standing over her with a torch, its dazzling beam making it difficult for her to make out any details of the intruder's appearance. He held her shoulders down on the bed and asked her for money; she pleaded that she had none. She cried out and he instantly stifled her plea for help, forcing a gloved hand hard over her mouth, telling her, 'Shut up, don't make a noise, don't tell anybody.'

She told him, with unwarranted politeness and under-statement perhaps, 'I think you are thoroughly mean.'

He began to search the bedroom by torchlight before returning to her, casting off the bedclothes and removing her underwear. He undid his trousers. He pushed his fingers into her vagina. He tried unsuccessfully to pull her legs apart; she later related that it had been 'incredibly painful due to my chronic arthritis'. He climbed on top of her and shone his torch in her face. She feigned illness and he seemed to give up on his attempts at rape, ejaculating on her lower body and legs. She was absolutely sure that he had not penetrated her. He got off and pulled the sheet and blankets over her and, in an incredible act of apparent concern, he then tried to find a pulse in her wrists, as if he were now suddenly bothered about her welfare.

The ordeal was over quite quickly, by Minstead standards, as the intruder spent just a few more minutes searching for loot before leaving empty-handed. His victim, grateful in many ways that she had not suffered more, did not immediately report the incident either to police or friends. However, as the daylight faded the following evening, she became apprehensive that the man might return and phoned her son. Surrey Police were called and arrived a couple of hours later. Her clothes were all taken for examination and of course she was medically examined and swabs taken. But it was the scientific examination at her home which was to prove most crucial: the key on a string was missing but it was discovered that, despite this easy means of entry, the intruder had at first attempted to force his way in through a window. In doing so he had used a screwdriver or similar implement which had left a distinctive 10-millimetre indentation mark on the frame. When photographed and recorded by making a cast of it this became a unique identifier – and one which was to prove extremely useful as he continued to use the same tool during several subsequent offences.

More important, however, was the examination of the lady's bedroom. A stain on the bedroom carpet – semen presumably either from premature ejaculation or perhaps masturbation – yielded a full male DNA profile. And although there was no match on the still-growing DNA database, it was identical to one which, due to improved scientific techniques, it had become possible to extract from the semen left during the 1992 offence in Shirley. An exact match between the crime-scene stains from the two offences told us that they must have been carried out by the same man. This definite linkage meant the offences were now, officially according to the service-level agreements between areas and divisions, a series. Despite the slight procedural difficulty of the two offences taking place in different police force areas, the criteria for making it a linked investigation within the Metropolitan Police were met. The arrangements meant that the series would be investigated not by divisional CID but by what was then known as the Area Major Investigation Pool (AMIP), a team dedicated to the investigation of homicide and other serious crimes, led by a detective chief inspector as senior investigating officer.

These AMIP teams were informally referred to as the murder squads, an epithet accurately reflecting the overwhelming bulk of their work. While their remit included other serious crime, it was relatively rare that they were so deployed. They were geared up for homicide investigations and were very good at it, regularly achieving a detection rate of more than 80 per cent, far exceeding the efficiency of the force in other types of crime. This success was due in no small part to their sheer numbers and an ability to throw all the resources of the Metropolitan Police and its scientific expertise into their enquiries. Add to that the fact that the staff were all experienced and proven detectives and it became clear they were a very effective force. There is no doubt that, when presented with the Minstead series, the expectation was that they would see a further success – and quickly. After all, there was DNA, making it a simple matter to prove the offences; the only issue would be finding the man who had left it. And that was what they were very good at. I am sure nobody, at that stage, dreamed it would be another eleven years until he was finally captured.

Chapter 5

IT BECOMES A 'STICKER'

As their impressive record of success suggested, the AMIP teams were not used to failing. Most murders being unplanned, spontaneous crimes they were surprisingly easy to solve. Easy, that is, if huge resources and all the most modern science available were thrown at them. The murderer had, in the majority of cases, not thought about forensics, CCTV, telecoms data and eye-witnesses. The AMIP teams had the ability to investigate these lines exhaustively and generally came up with the evidence.

This, then, engendered a mindset, a confidence among the officers that they were always likely to succeed – one which undoubtedly aided their efficiency. However, in hindsight this might also have been a handicap. The murder squads mentality also meant the default position was to investigate in this all-encompassing and forensic manner – and this may have dictated that in the Minstead case they follow a high-level strategy which was relied upon and maintained to the exclusion of more lateral thinking.

In the rare cases where early progress could not be made the investigation was informally referred to as a 'sticker'. In other words, the case had become difficult to progress and the team was stuck, both with the case and, to a degree, as to what they should do next. At the earliest stage it was considered that it was purely a matter of time. The suspect would show himself, either in a further offence which would itself present more opportunities to identify him, or by being arrested for an unrelated, possibly more minor, offence that would result in his DNA being taken and a match being found. As the old Met adage went, 'He will come.' But he did not. Operation Minstead soldiered on into 1999 without making progress, and in the summer of that year got a whole lot worse as the offending rate increased dramatically.

It started with an offence in Beckenham in the early hours of 20 June 1999, when a man broke into the house of a 71-year-old woman by removing a pane of glass from a rear ground-floor window. He found her asleep in her upstairs bedroom and roused her by leaning across her body, his sheer weight causing her to wake with a terrified start. She saw that he was dressed all in black, it was dark and the only other description she could offer was that he was a large black male. He put his hand across her mouth and nose, causing her to begin to struggle. His response was to subdue her by placing first one and then two pillows over her head. One can only imagine the fear she experienced at this, the very real prospect that an intruder was about to suffocate her in her own bed while she was powerless to resist him.

She stopped struggling and he removed the pillows, as he did so asking for 'diamonds and money'. He then began a search of her bedroom furniture by the light of a small torch. He then told her that he wanted oral sex from her. She asked to be allowed to get water from the bathroom and her attacker agreed. As he followed her she bravely turned to struggle with him, her strike missing its intended target of his genitals but knocking the torch from his grasp. As he scrabbled on the ground to retrieve it, she pleaded with him to leave her alone and to leave her house. Perhaps not expecting such a spirited response, he fled and, after waiting some time to be sure he had gone, the plucky victim tried to call for help. As was becoming the Night Stalker's trademark, she found he had turned off the electricity at the main fuse and pulled the telephone wire from its socket and so she was unable to call immediately for assistance, having instead to go next door. She had sustained severe bruising to her arm and swelling and cuts around her nose and mouth but said she was just grateful to have escaped with her life.

She found that the customary jewellery and around £100 in cash had been stolen, but when police later examined the scene they found that in his hasty departure the intruder had dropped the scarf with which he had shielded the lower half of his face. This was of course submitted for examination and subsequently yielded a DNA profile from saliva that exactly matched the profile from Shirley and Warlingham, confirming this was a Night Stalker offence.

I read next of another twist – what was at the time the first known attack on a man. In early July a widower of eighty-three who lived alone in a bungalow in Coulsdon, Croydon – partially blind and suffering from severe health issues which included Parkinson's disease – had retired to bed around 10 pm. He was awoken a few hours later by a dark figure sitting at the end of his bed with a torch, asking for money. The old man explained to the blurry figure that he had only about £5, whereupon the burglar dragged him out of bed and frogmarched him down to the hall where he took £17 from a small wooden box. He was then dragged back into his bedroom where the intruder started to punch him, hard and repeatedly, about the body. In pain from the volley of blows, the terrified man was then flung on to the bed. Forcing the old man's legs apart with his knee, the suspect indecently assaulted him by inserting fingers into his anus. The whole ordeal lasted for a couple of hours, the burglar searching all the rooms while the victim pretended to sleep, listening petrified and hurting on his bed. When he was happy the coast was clear, the man got up at 4.30 am only to find, naturally, that the lights were not working and his telephone line was dead. In agony, humiliated and unable to bring himself to try to walk to his neighbour, the man began to cry out with as much gusto as his aching body would allow. He was fortunate that his pleas for help were quickly heard and answered; the police arrived shortly afterwards.

They found that entry had been forced by removing a pane of glass by stripping the beading, that light bulbs had been removed and the phone wires cut. Marks on the beading were found, subsequently, to be identical to those made by the Night Stalker at the scenes of several other offences. The removed panes, the disabled lights, the disconnected phone lines, together with the clothing, the torch, the masking and the interaction with the victims after waking them from their sleep – it was clear, even from this handful of offences, that the Night

Stalker was a creature of habit and that his signature methods were already becoming very distinctive.

A few days later in July 1999 there was what would prove, in time, to be a rarity: a Minstead offence where the Night Stalker tried to break in but gave up. The exact date was unclear as it was not discovered for some time, but it took place at a bungalow in Orpington occupied by a lone 77-year-old woman. She found tool marks on the frame of the aluminium patio doors at the rear of her home, a series of small gouges giving the appearance that somebody had used a hard implement, most likely a large screwdriver, in an attempt to force the doors open. These marks were photographed and resin-cast impressions made of them which, when analysed later microscopically, proved conclusively that the tool used to make them was the same as the one used by the Night Stalker during offences where he had left DNA. That meant logically this was likely a Minstead offence too, albeit a lesser one of attempted burglary. Because the actual time of the attempt was not known it was impossible to say why he had abandoned it; whether he had been frightened off in some way or simply given up due to lack of success. Either way, it was a lucky escape for the lady who lived there – there can be no doubt that had he continued, she too would have come face to mask with the Night Stalker.

My research took me next to Addiscombe, again in Croydon, to a detached house where an 82-year-old lady lived alone. She had gone to bed around midnight on 11 July 1999 and was awoken shortly afterwards with a gloved hand over her mouth and nose. Upon opening her eyes she saw the dark figure looming over her, the eyes his only facial feature visible under a black balaclava. He told her he wanted money. The victim calmly told him she would not scream and that her money was in the wardrobe, in a handbag. He released his hand from her face, went to the wardrobe and pocketed the cash from the handbag. Going back to the bed he found the lady sitting on its edge. He sat down next to her, unhurriedly, and rested his head on hers, saying, 'Do you want to have sex?'

Stunned by the request she asked him to repeat it in case she had misheard; once he did, she explained serenely that she was an old woman and it really would not do anything for either of them. Undaunted, he pulled her legs apart, lifted her nightdress up and put his hands high between her legs, although not actually touching her vagina. She politely asked him not to hurt her, recalling later that the conversation was almost respectful, neither violent nor aggressive. She described his action as 'fumbling around' as she repeated her plea that he should not hurt her. She asked to use the toilet and he allowed this, then moved out to look in her other rooms aided by his torch. She followed him downstairs and saw him produce a can of John Smith's bitter from a pocket, which he opened and began to drink. The suspect then made as if to leave and the incredibly calm old lady opened the front door for him, thanking him for not hurting her as she did so. Remarkably, the intruder shook her hand as he left.

Once she had raised the alarm, having replaced the fuses from the box under the stairs to restore her electricity supply, police attended and found that the burglar had left his beer can on a table. From this a partial male DNA profile was subsequently obtained, one which although incomplete was entirely compatible with the known Minstead crime scene profile. Not that that was to matter too much, evidentially, as it was also discovered that he had entered by removing a panel from the back door and in doing so had caused familiar and matching tool marks.

Skipping a few crimes with sketchier details, I then turned the page to embark upon the most harrowing of all these incredibly disturbing reports. Once again it took place in Orpington, indeed in the very same road as the failed attempt to force the patio doors. But this 88-year-old woman was nowhere near as lucky. She had lived in her bungalow for twenty-five years, alone as her husband had died seven years prior to her moving in. She suffered a little from arthritis but refused to let it restrict her from leading an active, independent and fulfilling life. At three in the morning on Thursday, 5 August 1999 she was in bed asleep when she was woken by a noise. Looking up in the gloom, she saw a figure standing at the foot of her bed. She said the intruder was a man, completely covered from head to foot in what she described as a catsuit. She could see he had gloves and a balaclava on, and that he had a bright torch, which he was shining directly into her face.

He approached her at the side of her bed and, covering her mouth with his gloved hand, told her, 'Don't scream, I won't hurt you.'

Sadly, this time he was not true to his word. She asked what he wanted, he asked for money. She told him there was none in the bedroom, he would have to let her go to the living room to get it, so he pulled her to her feet. Grabbing her stick he bundled her into the living room where she took a purse from her handbag and gave it to him. The Night Stalker took the cash from the purse, discarded it and then focussed on her.

He dragged her across the small room from the armchair she had sat in, positioning her on the edge of a sofa. He pulled up her nightdress and proceeded to rape her, at least twice, both vaginally and anally. When, as she put it, he was satisfied, he went to the bathroom, returning with a towel which he threw to his battered and bleeding victim. He then started searching around the house, saying he had dropped a glove. Once this had been located he left the bungalow and the victim was able to raise the alarm using a 'Carelink' intercom installed at her home.

Paramedics as well as police attended and the woman was immediately removed to hospital, so serious were her injuries and her blood loss. She had to undergo emergency surgery for tears to her vagina and rectum, and a perforated bowel was among the severe injuries she sustained to her abdominal cavity. It was the closest the Night Stalker ever came to killing a victim there and then. She never returned to her tidy little bungalow that had been her home for a quarter of a century, being discharged from hospital to sheltered accommodation. And while her injuries were repaired and healed, her mind never did. The ordeal she had suffered inflicted psychological damage from which she was never to recover.

Crucially, semen found on her night dress yielded a full male DNA profile identical to the other Minstead offences. There was no doubt – this had been the Night Stalker's worst atrocity.

Between 29 June and 5 August 1999, twelve new Minstead offences were recorded by the team, half of them confirmed as linked either by DNA or tool marks or by both. The others were so distinctive in their method and features that they could not sensibly be discounted. However, this is not to say that every possible offence was, even at this early stage, accepted by the Minstead team for investigation. When in 2009 we looked back at all crimes reported more than ten years previously, applying more generous criteria it became clear that the scale of the Night Stalker's offending was much wider than had been thought. For example, between the first offence with DNA found in October 1992 and the second in September 1998 which created the 'series', it was possible to list a further thirty-two offences likely to have been committed by him, involving thirty female and two male victims aged between fifty-six and ninety-two. All these had been investigated by the appropriate local Borough police, the lack of DNA meaning there was no obvious scientific link. Somehow no thought had been given to the similar and unusual features suggesting a one-man crime wave – despite the reported offences being shared across just five Met divisions and Surrey Police. The existence of the series ought to have been determined – or at least considered – long before the second offence yielding DNA.

It took a moment for this to sink in. I went and made a coffee and wished in that moment that I hadn't given up smoking. Part of me – the loyal, proud, police officer part – hated feeling so critical of my colleagues. But mostly I was shocked. And angry. Because it was becoming clear to me that it might have been possible to nip the whole Minstead series in the bud.

Each one of those reported burglaries passed under the eyes of a number of officers and staff. There were the reporting officers who attended the scene and wrote the crime report; then the crime desk staff who screened it and allocated it for investigation. At least one officer would then investigate and he or she would have that investigation supervised, by a sergeant while it was live, and then by a more senior detective who would sign it off as complete. All the while an intelligence unit would be looking at everything going on within the division and an analyst with the explicit task of looking at crime patterns. I find it unfathomable how thirty-two offences of an unusual nature and with unusual features somehow passed all these people by, that one of them did not just think, 'Hold on, this is familiar, something is going on here.'

But the spree of offences stopped as suddenly and as unexpectedly as it had started. The last of them, the shocking attack on 5 August 1999 on the woman in Orpington, led to a greatly raised profile for Operation Minstead, both internally within the Met and externally in the media. Whether it was the publicity causing him to fear arrest or his guilt as to what he had actually done we may never know, but the Night Stalker went quiet and the offences took a temporary but (for us) much-needed halt.

And as, at this point in my reading, the office clock showed after 8.30 pm on a Saturday night, I decided it was a convenient place to stop and that I would return for the second phase of offences the following morning.

Chapter 6

GETTING UP TO SPEED – THE 2000s

It was unusual on a working Sunday to find myself alone. Most times interrupted weekends involved chasing round to new homicides on-call or leading the whole team on a search for a suspect. Otherwise Sundays were for dog walks, washing cars or watching sport. My only concession to the weekend being jeans and a T-shirt, I was once again embarking on a caffeine-fuelled review of horrific reports from years ago.

I ploughed into the cases again, first realising that by the time the offences were thought to have resumed, after a break of two years, lots of analytical work had resulted in a fairly solid set of features which had been listed as a guide for officers investigating burglaries. While it was stressed in the circular that not all had to be present (and in truth, *all* of them never were), this of course became as much a justification to exclude, as well as include, offences. The official list was:

- Meticulous pre- and post-offence preparation
- Telephone disabled (wires cut externally or internally or

pulled from socket, wireless handsets or mobiles
moved/hidden)

- Rear/side windows removed intact or forced
- Tools used from victims' or neighbours' sheds etc.
- Suspect will be gloved, masked (has used baseball hat
  or scarf instead of balaclava on some offences)
- Switches off electric mains or removes fuses
- Light bulbs removed, curtains drawn
- May spend some time in the house before locating
  victim
- Shines torch in victim's face
- Uses hands or body to control victim
- May spend some time with victim walking around
  the house looking for cash or jewellery (total time in
  premises can run into hours)

As I began to look at the horrid details I had these features
in mind and it became clear the analysts had chosen wisely.
The second phase of offences was thought to have begun on
Sunday, 13 October 2002, at a detached house, once more in
Shirley and home to a 75-year-old woman. On this occasion
breaking in was challenging for the Night Stalker and gave us
a good illustration of the man's tenacity. Not that getting into
the house was difficult – the by-now customary removal of a
whole pane of glass from a rear window saw to that. But he
then found his progress through the house barred by a locked
internal door. Patiently, almost incredibly, without waking the
sleeping occupier he had somehow chipped away at the wood
around the lock on the door until he had made a hole large
enough to insert his hand and release it.

The occupier woke up when she heard a noise in her bedroom. Taking a torch she always kept under her pillow, she illuminated the room and saw a man at the foot of her bed. She later said he was roughly 5 feet 9 inches tall, burly and a light-skinned black man. She recalled he had spoken with a local, London, accent when he informed her that he would like to tie her up. He then climbed on top of her and placed his gloved hand over her mouth, at which the lady bit him on the hand but thought this had little effect due to the thickness of the fabric of the gloves. She had found it difficult to see much more as the attacker began to shine his own torch directly into her face. She said he was very aggressive as he pinned her down to the bed by lying on top of her with all his body weight. The intruder, having tried to kiss the victim, forced his tongue into her mouth; at the same time she felt him putting pressure between her legs, trying to prise them apart. She resisted this with as much might as she could muster, fearing at this point that she was about to be raped.

While struggling so bravely she also had the presence of mind to begin speaking, calmly, to the man in the hope that she could yet defuse the situation, a tactic she maintained until the man had left the address. She had told him to get off and, although he was swearing at her and making unpleasant remarks about her personal hygiene, she pretended not to hear and kept up her gentle conversation. She offered him all the money in her purse, which was nearby in the bedroom, and thought that this seemed to appease him. He allowed her to get up and asked her to accompany him while he toured her house, looking for further valuables to steal. He then decided to leave. In doing so the victim promised him she would not call the police for ten minutes so as to allow him to make an escape. He responded to this by kissing her on the cheek as he left.

The spirited lady's cheek was swabbed and it resulted in strong evidence, a DNA profile from saliva on her cheek. There was no doubt, the Night Stalker was back. However, his rate of offending was nowhere near as prolific as it had been in the summer of 1999. A burglary took place in Catford in early March 2003 that was reported to the Minstead team because the victim was an eighty-two-year-old lady who was in at the time, entry was by removing a complete rear window pane and the fuses removed from the electricity supply. But as the victim was not woken up, there was no interaction with the suspect. He had simply stolen cash from the kitchen and left. On this basis the case was deemed not to be a Minstead offence and returned to the division for investigation.

Just two days later he struck again, this time in West Dulwich where a woman of seventy-eight lived in an end-of-terrace house. It had been her home for nearly forty years, the last eight years alone since her husband had died. Although she suffered with sciatica and walked with the aid of a stick she was an active, independent and reasonably healthy old lady.

Her habit was to sleep with her landing light on, but almost as soon as she woke up at about 2am she noticed it go off. Grabbing her stick, she ventured out of the bedroom in almost total darkness, determined to see what was going on. As she carefully inched her way downstairs into the hall she noticed that the telephone at the foot of the stairs was also not illuminated. She immediately thought it was a power cut; the truth of course, as had become the norm, was that the Night Stalker had switched her electricity off. As she fumbled in the darkness for a torch, she was suddenly aware of what she described as 'a huge black figure' looming over her. The figure pushed her over onto the ground, his gloved hand covering her mouth. At closer quarters she could see the man was, she thought, quite tall, maybe 5 feet 10 inches, with a broad build. He was wearing dark clothing, including a balaclava. But she was certain he was a black man. She wriggled and kicked and struck out with her hands but he was simply too strong and heavy for her to make any real impact. She did though, she was quite sure, manage to inflict a scratch or two on his face during the struggle.

Submitting to the inevitable, she offered the man her money, telling him where to find her purse. This caused him to release her and she sat alone in her living room and listened on as the burglar searched everywhere around her home. When he returned it was with a cloth, which he used to wipe carefully around her hands. He was likely fearing there would be DNA there from their struggles, though it was an unusual act for him – while he was super-careful never to leave fingerprints, we assumed he had been quite relaxed about DNA in the past as he knew we were unable to tie it to his name.

His clean-up was, though, insufficient. Scrapings were taken from under the lady's fingernails and, although for some reason it took the Minstead team more than two years to submit them for analysis (a quirk to which I will return later on), they eventually yielded a full male profile from skin cells which confirmed the burglar had been the Night Stalker.

Four more offences followed during July and August 2003, two each in Bromley and Croydon. None of these was tied conclusively to the Night Stalker and the frustration continued, but with victims aged between 78 and 89 years, there can be little doubt who was responsible.

The next three burglaries – on 21, 23 and 30 August, at properties occupied by women aged seventy-five, sixty-six and eighty-six respectively – had many Minstead hallmarks, and in the first two there was an indecent assault on the victim. The full scientific examination at each scene yielded extraneous fibres, in every case from the scene investigator taping (that is, dabbing the area with sticky tape to remove anything loose) near the point of entry. The fibres were a match for those left at an earlier Minstead scene where there was DNA, the offence in West Dulwich on 8 March 2003. But unlike the tool marks, fibres are rarely conclusive. Most clothing being mass-produced, it is not possible to be definitive about their source. Even if they are microscopically identical it is usually impossible to state definitively that they came from the suspect's clothing when there might be thousands of the same garment in circulation.

Like the fingerprint match with too few points of coincidence, or the partial DNA profile, it can be infuriating knowing that the science points strongly to your suspect but it is just not good enough for court.

There followed a relatively quiet spell, just four offences recorded in the next year, none of which yielded any hard evidence to connect the Night Stalker but all bearing tell-tale features and involving female victims over eighty. It was to be September 2004 before there was a case where his involvement was indisputable.

On 7 September 2004 he struck at the semi-detached home of an 84-year-old widow in Bromley. The report told a familiar tale. She was woken at about 2 am by a gloved hand being placed over her face, her shock compounded when she saw the figure looming over her, just a frightening outline with a bright torch. Then he asked for money, she pleaded with him not to hurt her and he allowed her to get up to use the toilet. As she emerged, he pushed her into the wall grazing her arm. As it began to bleed he told her get a plaster to put on it, which she did. I wondered whether this was out of compassion or his self-preservation instinct – did he want to avoid getting incriminating victim's blood on his clothing?

They went downstairs and the old lady showed him the drawer in her kitchen where she kept her savings, roughly £1,000 in cash. He took the money, one of his better hauls, and ran. When police arrived just after 3.30 am and found a removed window pane, cut telephone wires and bulbs taken from sockets, it was clear with whom they were dealing. A search of the area around the house was conducted and they found a glove, which was submitted for examination. Later a mixed DNA profile, containing the Minstead male profile and another from a female, was retrieved from inside where the fingers joined the palm. It was to be years later, after his arrest, that this glove was identified as belonging to Delroy Grant's girlfriend, but for the moment it didn't matter. This crime was obviously his.

I was nearing the end of my research. During the next four years there had been just around twenty further offences, none of them giving up any definitive evidence that they were the work of the Night Stalker but each with sufficient features to suggest it had almost certainly been him. A handful had fibre connections but no DNA or tool marks had been found. Fortunately, none of these victims had suffered any serious

57

injury – always bearing in mind that, even where he offered no violence or sexual touching, such was the nature of the crimes and their victims that every Minstead burglary left an elderly person deeply shocked – and in many cases psychologically scarred.

Reading through the post-millennial offence reports it became clear to me why the criteria listed as the signature of a Minstead offence had been chosen. The distinctive features of the crimes were not only very similar to each other but also very different from almost every other burglary. And a quick search on Google Street View for each one proved conclusively that he was indeed a creature of habit when selecting a home to attack. Most striking though was the interaction with the victim; something that most burglars did everything possible to avoid, this man seemed to relish. I could understand why the working theory was that this was a criminal seeking the interaction and sometimes sex, someone to whom the burglary might have been of secondary, almost incidental importance, just a means to get close to the elderly victims. Hence, 'We're not a burglary squad.' Was the suspect a weirdo who had a sexual thing about old ladies and only broke into their houses so he could be in their company?

Certainly, this was the major thrust of the publicity, of appearances on *Crimewatch* and internal briefings within the Met. I am sure that stressing the sexual nature of the offences and badging them all as such helped raise the public profile and grabbed more attention. I am equally confident that most of my colleagues outside of the Minstead team, as well as the public a large, were of the view that Operation Minstead was about a rapist, an atypical rapist who preyed on older women in their homes, but nevertheless a rapist. Which made it all the more likely, hindsight tells me, that the mindset was steered firmly towards snaring a rapist. And as always these days, a major chunk of the evidence in a rape case will be DNA evidence. I think it is possible that the characterisation of the offences also, perhaps subconsciously, steered the investigative strategy very much in the direction of finding a rapist, not a burglar.

Operation Minstead had had a shake-up or two, a change of staff and leadership, but what never seemed to change was that primary strategy. It really was all about the DNA – it was the only definite link not just between the offences but also to the offender. The simple truth was that there was little else to go on and, as this new method of identification and proof was solving more and more crimes, it is perhaps unsurprising that it became the mainstay of the Minstead investigation.

But recent police history has shown that DNA is by no means the panacea it was once thought to be. Thinking on this dragged me out of the immersion in the actual cases for an hour or so. I found myself thinking much more generally, the notes I was scribbling referred not to the individual reports but the overall strategy of how the investigation of major crimes had developed. I eventually came to the conclusion that we had all, in the excitement of science giving us a wonderful new method to solve our cases, allowed ourselves somewhat to get carried away.

Chapter 7

THE DNA SEDUCTION

L et us, like I did at least mentally, leave that office and take a break from the troubling details of the Minstead crimes to think a little more generally. There have been dozens of books and articles published on the use of DNA in investigations, all written by those far better qualified than me. I ought not try to give a scientific explanation of how it works; that is for the scientists. My experience of it is much like that of any detective – a user who has an appreciation of what it can mean and how it can be used. For that there is little need to have a really detailed scientific knowledge of how profiles are produced and compared, just of those instances where it is likely to be recoverable.

DNA profiling was developed during 1984 by a British scientist, Sir Alec Jeffreys, who found that an individual's DNA profile varied from virtually every other person alive, and so there was potential to use it for identification. The similarity with the discrimination of fingerprints was such that it was almost immediately dubbed 'genetic fingerprinting'. Within four years it was used for the first time in the UK during a Leicestershire Police murder investigation which resulted in the identification and conviction of Colin Pitchfork. An excellent explanation of that case is to be found in the book *The Blooding* written by the ex-LAPD cop Joseph Wambaugh in a non-fiction departure from his usual police procedurals.

The use of genetic fingerprinting grew gradually and it was not until the mid-1990s that a DNA profile was routinely taken from arrested persons in the UK. Consequently, the growth of a database against which crime-scene stains could be compared did not really take off until then, and DNA profiling would not really emerge as a mainstream investigative tool until the turn of the millennium. Since then, though, it has become widespread, used in a majority of serious criminal cases. Due in no small part to the public's seemingly insatiable appetite for true crime and crime dramas, the lay person is now acutely aware of this; indeed it has come to be expected as the norm in all cases. This can cause issues when prosecuting those few offences where no DNA evidence is available. The jurors have seen it in their televisual diet of *CSI* and *Dexter* and *Silent Witness* and the rest of them – there is *always* DNA. So, it has become necessary for prosecutors to explain its absence to them in some detail in order to head off a line of thinking that 'If he'd done it he would have left DNA' and so leading to erroneous acquittals.

As is to be expected, my view of the use and usefulness of the techniques comes very much from the perspective of somebody engaged in the strategic direction of major crime investigations. DNA profiling is at its most useful when you are trying to prove the presence of a person – whose identity is *known* to you – at a particular location. Or that *known* person was in contact with a particular object or even body. Such is the level of development of the science that it is now realistically possible to obtain a DNA profile from the merest touch. Techniques are available to 'grow' a profile from the smallest, most microscopic, trace of DNA-bearing material – as well as blood, sweat and tears, saliva, semen, hair roots or skin cells – all have the potential to leave genetic material. The sensitivity of these 'growing' processes means that in use they are not without issue – for example, contamination of samples by other persons has become a bigger issue and the scientists will often produce a sort of DNA soup, a mixture of profiles. They have though almost simultaneously developed processes to deal with this and to isolate from the mixture that which is relevant. A full DNA profile will give a probability of more than one billion to one that the material has come from anyone other than the matching individual. Barring anomalies such as identical twins, this is, for all practical and legal purposes, absolute certainty. Hence, in Minstead, we knew that as soon as we identified the suspect and matched his DNA to the profile recovered from the multiple crime scenes, he was sure to be convicted.

So, in proving presence or contact, DNA provides us with evidence so compelling that it is virtually unequalled. It is just as effective in identifying a known individual – where you have the suspect's DNA on file, on the (nowadays quite comprehensive) database of criminals, a match will be speedily found by the computers. Searching each profile is converted to a sequence of digits that powerful machines can compare in seconds – and then the investigators can find him, arrest him and, once another physical sample from blood or a mouth swab is taken from him to make absolutely sure of the match, the evidential power of the science and the statistics can come into play. All of which is what happens, day in day out, up and down the UK and indeed across the world. DNA profiling solves cases and convicts criminals, of that there is no doubt.

The difficulty arises when you have the situation in which Operation Minstead found itself. A crime-scene profile is recovered but when searched, no match is found on the national database. The investigator knows the potential of this, that the evidence will be there as soon as a profile is taken from the perpetrator. And this is where the seduction starts.

The temptation – especially in the absence of other leads or viable lines of enquiry – is to rely on this, to pin your hopes on the perpetrator's profile being added to the database and a match appearing during one of the regular runs where existing crime-scene stains are compared with new entries. Historically this is what has tended to happen – a good example is Mark Dixie, the chef who was convicted of murdering the model Sally Anne Bowman, in Croydon in 2005. Dixie's profile was not on the database at the time of the murder but almost a year later he got into a fight in a pub and was arrested for assault. His profile was uploaded to the database, quickly matched to the Sally Anne Bowman scene and the team had their man. However, when it does not work out neatly like this, when time marches on without the suspect surfacing from the computer, it is then that the thoughts of those leading the investigations turn to making something happen. And that, virtually inevitably, means they have to organise a mass-screening operation.

Mass-screening *can* work; indeed, two criminals I have referred to already – Pitchfork and Imiela – were each identified and convicted as a result of them. But they are not enterprises to be embarked upon lightly. First, they are inordinately resource-intensive: a normal-sized murder team engaging in a mass-screening will, unless significantly supplemented, have difficulty in completing other tasks and actions while they are chasing suspects to swab. Second, they rely greatly upon good-quality intelligence, complete databases and skilful analysis to produce the target list for the screening. It is an obvious truth – if the actual perpetrator is not on your target list then there is absolutely no chance you of swabbing him, even if (as is almost impossible) you manage to get a sample from every person on your target list.

Operation Minstead, of course, as I have mentioned, faced additional layers of difficulty because of the background of the suspect. The target list comprised exclusively men from a community where historically there had been considerable tension and mistrust, so that their cooperation could never be taken for granted and in many cases was just impossible to gain. Which created the tricky problem of how to distinguish between a refusal based on a lack of trust or some principled dissent, and one based on the guilt of the man whose profile was being sought.

My view has long been that mass-screening exercises were very much a tactic of last resort. I had firmly decided that I would be extremely reluctant to start mass screening until I had exhausted all other possible lines of enquiry. That principle is in some ways a perfect illustration of my main discomfort with DNA profiling as a whole – that it skews investigative action away from other methods. What I mean by that is that we now have an entire generation of police officers who have always had DNA available to them. Many see it not as the fall-back but much more the first line to be followed in any investigation. Not only that but the Crown Prosecution Service has come to demand it in many cases as the most important factor in authorising charges – they clearly also like the security and certainty of conviction it gives them when presenting a case.

And, of course, very often it works. Most especially in spontaneous or badly planned crimes of all descriptions, DNA will identify, prove and convict. My fear is that it has led to a degree of deskilling, that detectives and perhaps lawyers too are so used to using DNA that when it's not available or there is no known profile associated with a crime-scene stain, they are at something of a loss as to where to go next. Once the crutch of DNA profiling is taken away, are they still able to conduct an investigation or a prosecution without it?

Operation Minstead seemed to me to have taken the reliance upon the DNA to a new level, trying to wring every last possibility out of the crime-scene profile in their possession. The actions, almost always referred to as 'cutting edge', were entirely understandable and there is a decent track record of investigations cooperating with scientists to break new ground. And it isn't always as horribly expensive as one might imagine: academic researchers and indeed private industry have often given their services free or very cheaply to have the opportunity to devise new techniques, mindful of the peer acclaim and future profitability that successful deployment of them might bring. Therefore the attempts to glean physical features from the profile were, again, completely understandable and sensible things to do.

What really troubled me was that there was very little else –

every line of enquiry somehow came back to the DNA profile. I knew that what was needed was a pause, a step back and a reassessment, but even at this early stage of my review I knew that to do that I needed to be offering a credible alternative. And at that time I had no idea what that might look like.

Chapter 8

FIRST-HAND EXPERIENCE

When I got to the office early on the morning of 11 May 2009, PC Tony Brooks, one of the intelligence team and a very experienced Minstead officer, greeted me with the news that there seemed to have been what he described as a 'proper job' overnight. I thanked him, took the address down and pulled out my trusty Met road atlas to navigate myself to Princes Avenue, south Croydon.

As I drove into the street I noticed that it was what my weekend cramming session had shown me was a typical Operation Minstead road. Entirely residential, 1930s-built bungalows with the giveaway signs of little modernisation, intact front gardens, many not levelled for cars, and even hand rails by the front door evident on many. Suburbia, a mixture of young families and retired folk with the latter's homes easy to spot, a prime example of the Night Stalker's happy hunting ground.

Ethel was seventy-eight, she lived alone in her tidy detached bungalow. The garden and drive up to the detached garage were as they were in 1938 when it was built; no need for widening for multiple cars like the homes of her younger neighbours. The windows had been replaced, probably at some time in the 1980s, the uPVC units smarter and harder-wearing than their wooden forebears but offering far worse security. The garden had a large tree and lawn, with the original concrete path. The front door too was original, wooden with small panes at the top, painted an old-fashioned shade of mid-blue. The bungalow just shouted, 'old person lives here', an indefinable but clear message to which the Night Stalker was fully attuned. It was as typical a Minstead crime scene as could be found.

Since the Met, with its usual inertia, had so far failed to deliver on its promise of a police car for me, I was in my old and rather grubby Land Rover Discovery, but this at least meant there was room for a couple of officers to get in and brief me. They would possibly welcome a sitting break from the drudge of the house-to-house enquiries I had seen them conducting as I arrived. I warned them that their suits were likely to get covered in spaniel hairs but they smiled and shrugged their shoulders as they settled in to tell me the story.

They told me that the suspect had entered by forcing a small window at the rear using a sort of pitchfork he had taken from the shed in the rear garden of the next-door property. This reminded me of another feature I had spotted during my read-through – he would often use tools or garden implements stolen nearby, so much so that advice to secure sheds properly had been part of the crime prevention advice Minstead officers had previously offered the public. Of course it also meant, when he did this, that the chance of further tool-mark evidence linking to previous offences was lost. Was that another clever modification to his methods he had hit upon?

I looked at the bungalow and saw that access to the rear from the street was via a gate at the side. Whether it had been locked or not was irrelevant; it was less than five feet high and would have presented little obstacle to any man with a reasonable degree of fitness and mobility. He had then leant in and opened a larger casement window, carefully removing ornaments from the inside window ledge and placing them carefully and neatly on the sill outside – a classic Minstead trait. Another tell-tale trait was that he had taken Ethel's mobile phone and hidden it out of reach on top of a wall cupboard. The widespread adoption of cordless and mobile phones had forced this evolution of his techniques; he could no longer rely on cutting wires and so had taken to hiding the handsets where the victims could not get to them.

Ethel had been quite lucid and given a good account of what had happened. She was sure her bathroom light had been on throughout, so there was not total darkness and she had carefully taken notice of every detail of what the intruder had done. She had gone to bed at 9 pm and was awoken by the man sitting astride her on her bed, gently shaking her shoulders as she slept face down. He repeatedly asked her for her money; she repeatedly told him that she had none. Then the man had grabbed her breasts, both of them, and squeezed gently. Not a violent act, more of a caress, but one which terrified her.

He had asked her, 'Do you want more?'

And she had of course declined, pleading, 'No, no, no.'

He had then got off the bed and rummaged through her chest of drawers, quickly giving up upon finding only clothing and thankfully missing about £100 in a purse, which she had put away to save. While he had been searching the drawers she had frantically tried to find her emergency alarm pendant on her bedside table, not realising that the Night Stalker had seen it first and hidden it elsewhere in the bedroom. Instead, when he next left her to go and seek valuables in the kitchen she managed to find a torch with an attached siren in her bedroom, but he had returned and taken it from her before she had any chance to use it.

In total she believed he was in her home for more than forty-five minutes and remembered that the first time she had been able to check her watch after he woke her it was 4 am. She had asked him to fetch her Zimmer frame so she could use the toilet; he agreed to this and brought it for her. After she had been to the toilet she walked back into the bedroom and he had pushed her, very gently, back on to the bed and told her not to get up again, taking her Zimmer frame away.

Ethel was certain that he then left her house at 4.30 am. She then got up, went to the back door and locked it and fell asleep, not raising the alarm until about 9 am when, unable to find her mobile phone, she called her daughter from her landline, which perhaps unusually, was still working. The man had stolen around £20 in notes and coins, while terrorising an old lady who feared throughout the ordeal that she would be raped. She described him as a black man, aged between thirty and forty, with big dark eyes visible through a thick navy balaclava that covered the lower half of his face and so prevented any better description. He had worn blue woollen gloves and spoke with a soft London accent.

It was the first time I had learned the details of a Minstead offence in real time at the scene. I desperately wanted to see Ethel, on compassionate rather than investigative grounds. I wanted to see how she was, to reassure her that we would keep her safe now, to experience exactly how this brute we were chasing left his victims, but she had gone away to stay with friends. I went into the garden and looked around as best I could without disturbing the forensic team who were busy trying to gather evidence. As I looked through into the rooms – the window, the Zimmer frame both where the suspect had left them – I recalled every detail of the story I had just been told. I tried to imagine just how terrifying her ordeal must have been, how courageous she must have been to get through it – but of course it was impossible, in the cold, post-offence light of day to put yourself in her shoes. And that was when I was hit with the full weight of the fact that she was just one of scores, hundreds even, that the Night Stalker had subjected to such inhuman suffering. I looked around at the handful of officers, still trying to investigate the crime as thoroughly as any murder, despite their numbers being about one fifth of those who would normally undertake it. I wondered if they really felt that they were going through the motions. Carrying out their duties diligently, sure, doing all the things they were meant to, to the best of their abilities – but how many actually believed it would work? That, ultimately, it was worth it because it was likely to succeed? Because if I was tending to think that it was not after just a few days, how must they feel having been immersed in it for months or years with no breakthrough?

It was a tipping point for me: this was not just an administrative task to be undertaken, it was a live mission to find the man responsible. But to try to do so in the way we were, it struck me at that moment, was completely unsustainable – and it was very probably impossible.

Chapter 9

MINSTEAD LITE

Back in my little office at the end of the corridor, I battled against an almost overwhelming sense of depression. The apparent hopelessness of the task and the barbarity of the offences we were trying to prevent operated together to make my mood increasingly bleak. The piles of paper around me with post-it notes of every colour protruding from their edges, the pages and pages of my handwritten notes with arrows and bubbles and asterisks and exclamation marks. Each one represented a question I had asked, a problem I had posed. And at that instant I had no answers, not even the seed of an idea. It had taken me ten days, working flat out, to get to the position where I was at least aware of the enormity of the Minstead problem. That was, though, very far from understanding what had to be done, let alone devising a process for doing it. I knew I had struck the word 'hopeless' from my vocabulary but nobody would have been surprised if I had, at that moment, applied it to my task.

Thankfully a knock on the door snapped me back to reality

and standing there I saw Terry Keating. Terry was a retired detective who now worked as a civilian on the Serious Crime Review Group and we had worked together at Shooter's Hill back in 2002 on my first posting upon my return to the Met. A man of both great experience and almost tangible geniality and warmth.

'Morning, guv'nor, fancy seeing you here,' was his cheery greeting.

My reply of, 'Yes, fancy that indeed' was rather less enthusiastic.

Terry smiled and, noticing he was carrying a large cardboard document box, I asked what he was doing here himself.

'Just been going through the Lab submissions for Minstead, for the next review we are doing,' he replied, with an air of weariness and an emphasis on the word 'next'.

'Ooh, perhaps we should talk then,' I said, motioning towards the one spare seat in front of my desk that was not buried beneath piles of paper. Terry dumped his box on my desk as I reached to the coffee-maker I had salvaged from my office at Putney and selected a mug for him that at least had the cursory appearance of being clean.

Terry shared with me that he had stumbled upon some awful news. Every exhibit seized from a Minstead scene had, as usual, been submitted to the forensic laboratory accompanied always by a document, the imaginatively titled 'Lab Form 1', completed to describe the exhibit, its source and what kind of examination or testing was required. Once the scientists had worked their magic, they returned a report which outlined their work and recorded their findings.

The HOLMES database for the investigation was where all

this had to be recorded. Each document generated by the case had to be typed on to the system, in order that it became an entry in the database and gained a unique number which was used to cross-reference it in future documents. The intention was to make everything available for retrieval almost instantly using the system's powerful and customisable search functions. This only worked properly if all documents were indexed like this to a common standard, one which was drummed into the operators. Any departure from the conventions risked a connection not being made and reduced the usefulness of the database.

HOLMES was always to be regarded as a tool, a means to an end rather than the end in itself; nevertheless, accuracy and adherence to its conventions were essential for a very good reason. If an officer created a search, then he/she needed to have absolute confidence that the resulting output was correct; that there was nothing returned that should not have been and, perhaps more crucially, that nothing which should have shown up was missing.

At that time the HOLMES system was a standalone system that was in truth rather old-fashioned. It did not allow attachments to documents. The work-around for this was that a physical box file would be registered on the system with its contents being described in text. This allowed for the existence of photographs, videos or images to be noted – and searched on – but the searching officer would then have to go to the box file and examine its contents to see the actual exhibit. Due to this restriction, the exhibit's content could not be discovered by a HOLMES search. In order to fit within the HOLMES system, the box file itself was registered as a document, so for example Document D1150 might be described as 'file containing DVD of CCTV from the Black Horse 29-11-2007' or similar.

What Terry Keating had found was that all the Lab forms for Minstead had been treated as if they were photos or videos, simply stored in a numbered box, rather than the text of each one being typed into the system as a separate document. So, there was one document, say it was numbered D16452, which appeared on the system named as 'Lab forms submitted' and the cardboard box he had been carrying, well, *that* was D16452. Inside was a whole host of Lab forms, going back many years, the contents of which were completely unknown to, and unsearchable on, the database.

This took a few moments to sink in.

'So, if I want to search HOLMES for, say, submissions of bedclothes to see how many we have results from, I can't?'

'Correct,' Terry replied, his expression showing he shared my despair. 'The only way you can find that out is by coming to the box and going through every single form, manually.'

I was trying to reply while at the same time my mind was racing away, trying to imagine the ways in which this might hinder our cause. And worse, what similar horrors might yet lie in wait?

I eventually broke the silence with a question to which I did not really expect an answer.

'Why, Terry? Why would they do it like that?'

But I did get an answer, one which was to direct my thinking for the next few days.

'It's numbers, Colin. All about the numbers. Basically, there is so much work and so few people to do it, the whole thing would fall over if shortcuts were not taken. Nobody wants to do stuff like this I am sure, but sometimes there's just no choice.'

While I had not found any evidence of this shortcut causing problems, it held the potential for a grave error. And it shook my confidence in how reliable the whole datatbase might prove to be. It did, though, focus my mind on the staffing levels, the mismatch between them and the workload, and so the current practices. This seemingly innocuous filing error was in fact indicative of two very serious issues with the Minstead team: lack of people and lack of motivation. In that sense it was very much turning point number two. To explain its relevance I need to fill in with a bit more of its recent history.

The Minstead team was, quite logically, set in the branch of the Met called SCD1, the Homicide and Serious Crime Command, which had been created to replace the old AMIP system. The overwhelming majority – more than 95 per cent – of cases investigated by this command were homicides, but it did retain a responsibility to take charge of some other cases, notably serial rape cases – which of course was where Minstead fitted in. However, the structure of the Command was, as one would expect, designed for its core business.

The Homicide Command divided London into three sub-commands: East, South and West, each of which had geographical responsibility for homicides committed in its area. These were, roughly and if the city were imagined like a clock face, from 12 to 3 East; from 3 to 8 South and from 8 to 12 West, with West also covering all of the City of Westminster. When I had joined the Command, in late 2002, each of these three areas had nine separate investigation teams, one of which had to be on call at all times, and so there was a nine-week rota for that duty.

I recalled that, some time around 2006, the then Commissioner Sir Ian Blair had decided that the size of SCD1 should be reduced as there was clearly room to continue to be reasonably effective with a smaller workforce. His reasoning, difficult to fault in truth, was that the murder rate had fallen and our detection rate was very high at around 90 per cent. So to free up posts to assist his push to bolster neighbourhood policing he would require the teams to slim down so the shed posts could be redeployed.

For most of us on the teams, the result was not too noticeable. We lost a couple of officers by natural wastage who were not then replaced but the only real difference was that, since each area was reduced to eight teams (for a total across London of twenty-four), our on-call duty now came every eight, rather than nine, weeks. What most of us – at least those not directly involved in the hunt for the Night Stalker at that time – did not realise was that even these cuts didn't quite add up to enough to meet the Commissioner's request for staff. In order to make up the numbers, it fell to the extra, twenty-eighth, team to suffer a disproportionate cut, reducing its strength by a half. That team, of course, was Operation Minstead.

In many ways this decision was completely understandable: perhaps the most compelling reason was that the cuts were asked for in 2006, during a very quiet period when new Minstead offences were most infrequent. It was a time when, even if the investigation had not been totally forgotten, it was certainly not at the front of the minds of those who were responsible for making the choices. What it did though was to remove any possibility of resilience, probably quite accidentally; to ensure that Minstead was consigned to be just about managing – and to mean that when offences started to become more regular, there was simply no spare capacity to respond to them.

The lack of numbers was compounded by the way in which staff were posted to the team. Most had recently joined the Command, having been selected thinking that they were joining a murder squad, since that was essentially what they had applied for. Very, very few, if any, ever submitted their application specifying that they were interested in joining Operation Minstead. While there is no doubt that, objectively, the Minstead investigation was every bit as important as any homicide – and almost certainly, from my experience, more challenging than most – it was obvious that many of the recently recruited felt real disappointment that they were not strictly in the role they had sought or coveted. The robust response to this would be that they should do as they were asked, and to some extent this was true. But already I had been able to see a side effect of this. During the meeting at Simon Morgan's house and again around the Lewisham offices I had, on several occasions, heard the phrase, 'We're not a fucking burglary squad' – often following, 'We aren't doing that...' It was said so often and by so many people I realised it was a sort of unofficial Minstead mantra.

While this was possibly desirable, encouraged even by some, to differentiate the team from those performing less glamorous and less specialised work elsewhere – and in so doing to reinforce their status as members of an elite command – it also betrayed a mindset that I feared was almost certainly not helpful. By the way in which the team was responding, it was evident its members were aping the methods used by their colleagues on the homicide teams. But they were quite obviously drowning in a sea of repeated offences and the mass of paperwork these generated, unable to make real progress because of the lack of staff to assist. They were trying to work just like a murder squad, but those squads took on a new investigation every six weeks or so at the soonest. They were often dealing with one or two a day, with half of the resources. And then repeating this the following day. One morning, the very worst, there were five overnight offences to respond to. It was therefore inevitable that they were beginning to go under. And tired, overworked police officers quickly lose their edge and effectiveness. I knew this all too well.

'Maybe they ought to be a fucking burglary squad,' I thought. 'After all, they are trying to catch a fucking burglar.'

Something had begun to dawn on me. Much of the work undertaken at the crime scenes was aimed at preserving and gathering evidence of the crime – exactly what one might expect of detectives responding to and investigating serious crimes. But was that really the objective? The circumstances of Operation Minstead were unique in that there was so much strong, historical evidence of the earlier crimes in the series. We did not, I realised, actually need to prove any of the new offences. There was firm and reliable DNA evidence from the old offences. The gravity of those offences would ensure that, once caught, the Night Stalker would go to prison for a very, very long time for those – even if there was no way of proving what he had done in the last five years. We did not need evidence that he had committed the new offences to put him away; all we needed to do was to find out who the hell he was. And thus was born the concept of 'Minstead Lite'. I appreciate that is a horribly corny name, but I never tried to improve upon it. What we called it was not important – what mattered was what we did and how it could make us work smarter.

The basis of my plan was that all new offences reported going forward should be treated not as crimes to be fully investigated but as intelligence opportunities. What we had to do first, as always, was to ensure we were caring for the victims and providing whatever support we could for them. Beyond that, the only thing we needed to do was try to exploit any aspect of the offence that might enable us to identify the perpetrator. This would involve some examination of the scene for scientific evidence and some local enquiries. But unless any of these appeared to be fruitful then there was no need to progress them formally, to take statements or to generate all the wide-ranging and comprehensive actions and bureaucracy that the current, murder squad-based, approach required. If we could reduce the workload substantially then we might be able to focus our efforts on the aspects most likely to lead to the one thing which would stop the Night Stalker's reign – finding out his name.

I thought I now had the basis of a plan. Devising it had been hard enough, but now I knew I was going to have to try to make it fly with those both above and below me who, I feared, might be hugely sceptical.

Chapter 10

REPORTING BACK

I had not really thought about how exactly I would report my findings and my plan to DCS Hamish Campbell – and he had not stipulated how I should explain my findings to him. My preference was for a face-to-face verbal briefing, but I knew the way in which the Met worked well enough to know that something tangible, on paper, was always going to be needed too. So, backing it both ways, I compiled a report but did not simply email it to the Yard, instead booking a meeting with the boss and taking a hard copy along.

Given that the report would undoubtedly be forwarded up the chain, possibly to the very top given the Commissioner's interest in the case, I ensured that it was factual, neutral, non-judgemental. But it had to make it plain what the struggles were and how they might be overcome. I outlined the strength of the team, comparing it to the workload it was battling against, and stated that a method needed to be devised which reduced the mis-match. So as not to appear entirely critical, I had kept any thoughts about the current strategy and objectives to myself. Not that I should have expected they would remain unvoiced for long.

My meeting with Hamish Campbell started in an unusual way. Sky News was, as ever, being silently broadcast on the large television screen on the wall of the SCD1 main office at Scotland Yard. As I entered, they were showing live pictures from a police raid being conducted by the Territorial Support Group, battering doors while seeking out drug dealers in some rundown part of London. Everybody in the office had their neck craned upwards towards the screen. It was slightly surreal and warmly encouraging that, here in the beating heart of the Met, officers and staff of all ranks were awestruck, concentrating without speaking as they watched their colleagues in action, live at the sharp end.

Hamish was standing at the entrance to his office, hands on hips, paying rapt attention to the TV. He heard me enter and turned towards me, motioning at the far wall and whispering, 'Bloody good stuff this.'

As the pictures changed from raiding officers to the presenter and a pundit in the sterile security of the Sky studio, Hamish turned on his heel and strode into his office, inviting me to follow with a cheery, 'Come on then, what have you got for me?'

I sat in the immaculately tidy office and began. As always, I had rehearsed how the conversation would open a thousand times in my mind, so when I handed my senior officer a copy of the report his response was exactly as I had expected.

'Yes, yes, I'll read that later, of course I will. But tell me about it, tell me what you think beyond the facts there on the paper.'

And so I did. I explained that there seemed to me to be two

factors which were limiting the likelihood of success: most importantly that the team was far too small to be effective. That could be addressed, in the short term at least, either by increasing their numbers (which I knew was unlikely to be possible) or by changing the way in which they worked. I had therefore devised changes to working practices to address this and they would be my recommendation.

But the second factor was much more difficult to deal with. Even if we implemented 'Minstead Lite', I was still by no means certain that it would be successful. It might allow an acceleration in the rate of screening DNA swabs obtained while at the same time providing a response to the reported new crimes, which in turn might disclose our quarry's identity. But 'might', as they say, was doing an awful lot of heavy lifting in that prognosis – we would have to be lucky and might be almost completely reliant upon the Night Stalker making a mistake. And that was something which, to date, he had showed absolutely no sign of doing.

Hamish considered this for a moment and then looked me in the eye.

'You aren't convinced this is the way forward, are you?'

'I think it's better than what we have at the moment,' I replied, knowing immediately that I had answered in a politician's way, avoiding the direct question – which would only provoke the further probing it deserved.

'What do you really think? Come on, if you were starting from scratch how would you go about it?'

While this was a question I had expected and to a degree rehearsed, it was one to which I still hadn't been able to prepare a satisfactory answer.

87

'I really haven't been able to come up with a plan for that, not in two weeks. I'm sorry, sir, but it all seems too complex for quick fixes.'

The DCS nodded sagely, showing that he was in agreement and perhaps, I thought, with relief that I had not leapt to judgement that there was a simple solution. So, I tried to expand.

'Remember when we could still make jokes without offending the persistently offended? There was a story about a tourist in the west of Ireland who stopped and asked a farmer the best way to drive to Dingle. He got the reply, "Now, to be honest, if I were you I wouldn't start from here." Well, that's kind of where I think we are.'

Hamish smiled. 'Where would you like to start from then?'

I was not at all sure that I knew, other than it being not where we were. I thought that the best way of progressing was, essentially, to think out loud:

'OK, we have DNA. Everything is about the DNA – I even wrote that to myself in the first meeting I attended.

'That has slanted every line of enquiry they have followed. Not just the mass screening but also the scientific work, the attempts to get information from the profile. Now you and I know how difficult a mass screening is to carry out successfully. I don't think it is putting it too strongly to say it's a tactic of last resort; that you only do it if there is no other viable alternative…'

The silent nod I then received was a little ambiguous – did my boss agree or was it just an indication that he understood my point of view? Either way, I had started so I needed to press on.

'I think there is a danger that so much has been invested in those lines of enquiry that it has become unthinkable to change it. I am sure if I had been following it so far and for so long, I would think that way myself. But, as an outsider looking in, well, I'm just thinking there might be another way.'

Hamish nodded again, this time in unmistakable agreement.

'That is precisely why I sent you over there, to apply a degree of fresh thinking which those so embedded in the investigation simply cannot.'

I felt relieved, supported and valued – and I also knew that I had much more to do. I knew now that it would be possible to effect a change, to redirect the enquiry to a course which I thought stood more chance of success. The glaring difficulty I faced was that while I had the opportunity, I had no real idea, at that point, how I could take advantage of it. It is one thing to say that the current plan is not working but something entirely different – and more difficult – to come up with a new one which would. And there was another elephant in the room which needed to be aired.

'It isn't easy for me, sir. I haven't got any real status on the investigation; if the direction is to be changed it can't really come from me, can it? It's so difficult, Simon Morgan has invested so much time, energy and passion into Minstead. I feel for him, I really do, he's in great pain and is soldiering on as best he can. If it weren't for his attachment to Minstead I am not sure he would still be working at all. How can I come in and tell him that I think it should all be changed?'

'It is indeed a very difficult and unusual situation,' Hamish replied with grave sincerity. 'We can't go in and rubbish everything Simon has done. But we will find a way, a way to move things on, I am sure.'

I told Hamish I felt bad. Worse than bad, awful. There he was, a fellow copper, fellow detective, doing his very best to solve an extremely difficult case with minimal resources and all the time battling against severe health problems – and here I was, raking over his work and seemingly plotting with a senior officer to find a way to change everything he had put so much time and effort into. The senior officer put me right there and then.

'We will make sure we look after Simon Morgan. We can't just rip his investigation from under him, it wouldn't be fair. What you need to concentrate on is going back and coming up with a viable alternative plan.'

We shook hands and left it at that.

Hamish did read the Minstead Lite document, as did Simon Morgan. Both agreed that it was sensible and that it gave the team some breathing space to cope with their overwhelming workload. I was very relieved and slightly surprised that my plan had been so well received. I hadn't so much feared that it was unworkable but more that suggesting absolutely any change might not be welcomed. I hoped they had realised that if they wanted a whitewashed, 'all is going fine' type of review they had come to the wrong man. It was implemented with an important additional provision, one which I added after my meeting with Hamish Campbell.

During our general conversation about the Minstead team's workload I had mentioned, almost casually, that one of the measures taken to try to make it more manageable was the very strict screening policy. The intelligence desk had a comprehensive search term which, when run every morning, returned any likely Minstead offences which had been reported in the previous twenty-four hours. This search covered all of London and the Home Counties but, tellingly, only ever disclosed crimes in the south-east quarter of London. One, perhaps the broadest, interpretation of this data was that the Night Stalker really was the only one committing these offences – and that he was obviously a creature of geographical habit.

However, if that were so then the frequency of his offending meant a workload impossible for the team to deal with. So while some offences were taken on by the team, many others were 'screened out' and returned to the local Borough CID to investigate. This was possible due to the lengthy list of unusual features in the Night Stalker's methods. As I have outlined, a list of twenty or so exceptionally rare features had been devised. While, obviously, not all of these were present at all offences, they had come to be regarded as the tell-tale signs of a Minstead offence. But as his offending increased they were, as a matter of desperate expediency, used for the reverse purpose: their absence was used as justification for returning the crime to Borough.

This troubled me greatly, as I knew that analysis of crime patterns was only as good as the information upon which it was based. The familiar phrase is 'garbage in, garbage out'. If we were rejecting offences as not the Night Stalker when in truth they were his work, then we would be skewing any such analysis. This might, depending upon how the course of the investigation developed, prove a barrier to success.

I wanted to add a further feature to the Minstead Lite scheme so that all offences reported to the team would be adopted for investigation unless it was absolutely clear from all the circumstances that the perpetrator could not have been the Night Stalker. If Minstead features were present the presumption would be that it should be taken for investigation unless there existed strong reasons not to do so. While this would undoubtedly mean more investigations being undertaken, that indeed was the aim. I considered the new methods might make this manageable and that the increased accuracy of our analytical work was a benefit which, in the longer term, we could not do without. In hindsight, given how the investigation methods were destined to change longer term, this was to prove one of my most important decisions, both in terms of aiding his capture and in portraying accurately the scale of his offending.

However, I knew that I would have to present some hard evidence to show that this was a necessary step. That would almost certainly mean a painstaking look back at offences returned to divisions for investigation, in the hope of finding compelling reasons to say that some of the Night Stalker's offending was being turned away by the Minstead team.

Fortunately for me I did not even have to embark upon that lengthy process. Proof came along and fell into my lap without my having even to start to try and find it.

Chapter 11

'HOW LONG CAN WE KEEP ON DOING THIS?'

Just a couple of days after my briefing and before Minstead Lite became the normal team procedure, some new information showed how the policy of including all allegations might be justified.

During the early hours of Monday, 25 May 2009 a burglary took place in a house in Farnaby Road, Bromley. The occupiers were an 88-year-old woman and her 62-year-old son. The burglar had approached the house from the rear, having climbed across a couple of neighbouring garden fences to make it there – so it was clear he had targeted this particular house. Having forced entry through a window and searched the house, he had, it seemed, moved some items around inside but had not actually stolen anything. Due to the age of the victims, the time of the offence and the location, the officers attending the crime quite rightly reported it to the Minstead team. Applying the strict screening criteria, the case was returned to the Borough for investigation, the rationale being that the Night Stalker always interacted with the victim and that he never selected as targets a property with more than one occupier.

The Borough had taken on the investigation diligently and their scenes examiner attended. She had swabbed the mouth of a Tesco 'Finest' orange juice carton, because of a remark made by the son of the occupier. He had noticed that the volume of juice in it had apparently decreased overnight and he therefore suspected the burglar might have taken a drink from it. This had real promise, since a previous offence had been confirmed as a Minstead crime from DNA left by the Night Stalker on a beer can to which he had helped himself.

This attention to detail paid off as within a couple of days the swab from the carton had yielded a DNA profile – and it was an exact match for the Night Stalker. Here was my proof – if the DNA had never been discovered this offence would have been ignored. I now had firm evidence that if we carried on screening out possible offences, we were undoubtedly going to miss Night Stalker offences – and the intelligence and analysis opportunities they might bring.

Obviously the Farnaby Road investigation was swiftly retrieved from the Borough. When we took over the investigation we found that a neighbour across the road had installed CCTV to cover his drive, on which he had parked a couple of expensive cars. It was low-quality equipment and the product was a bit blurry; also, aimed as it was at the Audi and the Porsche, it showed only the bottom half of passers-by. Nevertheless, analysis of the footage told us a couple of interesting things. First that the Night Stalker had walked some distance to the house that he had attacked, from the direction of the nearby Ravensbourne railway station. Did he travel to his crimes by public transport? Because if he did that was a whole new potential line of enquiry, the railways and buses having ample and sophisticated CCTV systems. Sadly, we soon found out that the last train through Ravensbourne station was a long time prior to his arrival on the scene, so there was no point in wasting resources on another speculative theory.

More importantly though, the timing of his approach and his much later departure gave us an indication of the Night Stalker's dedication to his work. He had passed the camera and therefore presumably entered the rear gardens more than three hours before he left the scene. By comparing the times of his sighting with the account given by the son of what had been going on in the house, it was clear that the Night Stalker had been sitting for more than two hours, unseen, watching from the garden – presumably waiting for the lights to go out to indicate that his intended victim had to gone sleep. Never before had the 'Night Stalker' nickname seemed more appropriate.

Despite the feeling of elation on the team that we had a new offence we knew was definitely the work of our suspect, even that we now had grainy images of his legs, I was unusually downbeat. All this had really proved to me was that the screening criteria were hugely fallible. If the Night Stalker had not quenched his thirst and left DNA, then this offence would not have stayed on our radar. I couldn't help but wonder how many more had slipped through the net. My justification for screening nothing out was, though, nicely formed and incontrovertible. I soon found that my subsequent request to include this rule in Minstead Lite was pushing on an open door.

My father's seventieth birthday was looming and we had agreed to host a barbecue for him and some friends at home. On Saturday, 6 June I went with my wife Louise to a cash and carry in Purley Way, Croydon to stock up on drinks and food for the birthday party. It was a bright sunny day, quite warm for early summer, and although I casually joked that as we passed the Croydon Borough signs that they should also say 'You are now entering Minstead country', work was far from my mind. It was the weekend: T-shirt and jeans, do our shopping and back home for a relaxing walk with the dog.

Almost inevitably, as we left the store and were loading the goodies into the old Discovery, my phone rang. It was DI Nathan Eason, so I immediately expected that my weekend of domestic peace was to be cut short.

'Sorry to bother you, Colin, but we've had another one, in south Croydon. An 82-year-old woman, a burglary where she was indecently assaulted too. She is suffering badly from dementia and it is, er, a little difficult to work out exactly what has gone on.'

'OK, have you got enough people?'

My question received the answer I should have known it would: 'When do we ever have enough? Not really, it's the weekend, so only a few are on. We can't keep calling them in on overtime…'

I looked at Louise; I could see in her face she knew what was coming; her own experience of policing was such that she always understood what the role demanded of me.

Looking at her with a half-smile I offered, 'OK, well, I'm not far off. I'll pop over and I can lend a hand.'

I asked Nathan for the exact location, looked up Queenhill

Road in the A–Z and navigated Louise through the unfamiliar streets of Croydon. I suggested she drop me off, reassuring her that I would not be long and that I could get a lift back to Lewisham and then grab a police car to get home.

We got to the scene after ten minutes or so and saw the familiar cordon tape with uniformed officers guarding against unauthorised entry and logging those who were to be admitted. I did not notice that they were all female but Louise obviously did. As I went to get out, she reached into the back of our car and picked up a light beige anorak of mine from the seat.

'Here, you'd better put this on,' she said with quite uncharacteristic insistence.

'No, I won't need that, it's lovely out there and I'm not going to be that long,' I said dismissively.

Louise looked me in the eye and sternly said, 'Look over at those officers, look down at your T-shirt and then tell me that you don't need the coat. Zipped up!'

I saw the women officers and then realised my T-shirt was a jokey printed item, featuring an unmistakable image of the *Life on Mars* TV character DCI Gene Hunt, with the caption: *Not now love, grown-up talk.* Definitely not a good look for a senior officer approaching a whole bunch of female officers. 'Thanks, Louise,' I thought, nodding my appreciation as I did the jacket up tightly to my neck and left the car to enter the fray.

Queenhill Road was, once again, classic Night Stalker territory: 1930s-built semi-detached houses, a few with their neat gardens, unmodified windows and general lack of modernity betraying their long-term and ageing occupants. Unusually for a Minstead scene, there was a car – a newish

Renault Clio – on the drive of number 18 where the attack had taken place. I remarked to Nathan that this was not normal and reminded him that in one of our brainstorming sessions we had discussed whether as a preventative measure we could try to get people to leave their cars on the drives of their vulnerable and aged neighbours, as we hoped it might dissuade the Night Stalker from believing they were alone. Nathan explained that the alarm had been raised by the victim's home help when she had attended that morning and it was to the care worker that the car belonged.

The poor lady's general confusion made it very difficult to imagine that she would be able to give us the key to unlocking the case we so desperately craved. To some perhaps it will be a surprise, but this was not our regular experience with the elderly. I had been keen to explain to the Minstead team a fact I had learned during the 1990s when dealing with a series of despicable distraction burglaries practised on the elderly in north London: the elderly turn out to be far better witnesses than many would imagine, every bit as good as those half their age or less. It is just that they remember different facts. So where the young witness will notice clothing, trainers, jewellery – all the things that 'make' a person in their eyes – older people are far more likely to note physical features such as eye or hair colour, complexion and accents. They are not worse witnesses, just different in the features they notice and therefore retain – and which enable them to remember people.

However, when the victim suffers from dementia it really becomes an almost impossible task to elicit useful information. Debbie Akinlawon and Sam Patterson, the ever-sympathetic and utterly dedicated Minstead family liaison officers (FLOs), were doing their usual very best but with no success. Nathan had noticed that across the road there was an entry to a tennis club. He suggested we go over and see if it had held a function the previous night, as this might yield a pool of potential witnesses. It seemed a reasonable punt, so I joined him. Although the lone barman was welcoming and even offered us a drink (for which, I am sure, we both had the appetite but sadly not the time) there had been nothing special going on the previous evening and so only a handful of members were there, all leaving just after 11 pm. We walked back down the alley towards the street. A sunny Saturday lunchtime in suburbia, marred by fluttering blue-and-white tape, police vehicles and a small band of dedicated detectives, scurrying about their task, which my heart knew would almost certainly be in vain. Nathan and I sighed, coincidentally, in unison. We stopped and turned towards each other. It was obvious in his expression that we were having very similar thoughts; I was the first to try to articulate them.

'How long can we keep on doing this?' I asked, knowing fully that my DI would understand what the 'this' was.

'I don't know, Colin,' he replied, his voice heavy with despondence. 'It takes pissing in the wind to a whole new level.'

I nodded, shrugging resignedly. 'Every time we are just hoping in vain this will be the one where he slips up. But he doesn't. So we wait for the next, then the next and so on. And every new one is another old lady terrorised and abused. We can't just keep chasing his shadows like this.'

'What's the alternative though, Colin?'

'We need to get in front of him, not be behind him all the time.'

Nathan grimaced and exhaled. 'Proactivity? They've tried it before, I think. Before my time here though…'

'Well, I think we need to look at it again. Because, to be brutally honest Nathan, this is utter crap. I'm sorry, but I really feel, well, if this is the best we, as the so-called elite detectives of the Metropolitan Police, can manage…' I tailed off mid-sentence, unable for the moment to grasp the words to express the powerlessness I felt in that moment, the futility I saw in what we were supposedly trying to achieve.

'Come on, give me a lift back to Lewisham, Nathan. Let's have a think about it and see where we are on Monday.'

Despite my assurances to Louise earlier on it was indeed late evening when I got home. She teased me that I was glad of the jacket after all and left me to my own devices, sensing that I had so much going on in my head that any attempt at conversation or other ordinary family life was pointless. I had spent a good two or three hours back at the office going through policy documents and other records. And then just sitting on my own in the dimly lit office and thinking. Yes, proactivity – trying to get ahead of the Night Stalker rather than just responding to his crimes after they were committed – had been tried a couple of times before but, as was so often the limiting factor in Minstead, the resources hadn't really been available to do the job properly. A few extra officers and vehicles, patrols in defined areas and hopeful stops conducted on passing black men. It occurred to me that the Night Stalker was probably much too canny to be caught that way.

I remembered my time as Head of Force Intelligence in West Yorkshire in the late 1990s. In trying to mount surveillance on proper, top-tier, cunning and aware criminals we had a basic principle that said that we must leave no trace, we must not disturb the status quo in any way. Nobody must know, or be able to work out, that we are there. At that time, we had had the advantage of numbers and the very latest technology to help us – and we were usually successful. If we were to get ahead of the Night Stalker then we needed to work to the same standard.

The first thing that needed to change was that Minstead mantra 'We're not a fucking burglary squad!' Because, as I had said to myself earlier, 'Do you know what, we are trying to catch a burglar!' Albeit one who occasionally rapes and often abuses. An unusual burglar, sure, but still a burglar.

This might be a hard sell to some of the team, I feared, but that was a battle I was prepared to fight and one that I was confident of winning.

Chapter 12

ELLEN

I am often asked whether the sort of work I did ever got to me. By that I am sure the questioners mean, 'Did dealing with death and depravity so close up for so many years affect you at all?' My usual answer is, truthfully, that it did not. I accept I am lucky that I was always able to compartmentalise my life; work was work and home was home. The most important people to me have always been my family and my friends – and the latter group are almost exclusively people I met as a schoolboy, not as a policeman.

The fact that I can do this is perhaps unusual – the issue of the stress placed on police and other emergency workers by the nature of their jobs is one which is only just being appropriately recognised. Steps are afoot to address this real problem for those who protect us and it is long overdue. But me? Perhaps sadly, at an early stage of my career I became very cynical about the incredible tendency of some humans to do unspeakable harm to others. My means of dealing with it was the ability to understand that this was their life and nothing like mine was – or would ever be. Savage thinking, perhaps, but effective.

However, there were just a few occasions when the outright sadness and unfairness of the things I encountered tested this ability severely. Speaking with the parents of murder victims like Amélie Delagrange and Marsha McDonnell were such times – the sheer brutality of senseless violence intruding, irretrievably, into their ordered lives was horrible to witness and impossible to ignore. On Operation Minstead, the victim that breached my wall of stoicism was Ellen. (Not her real name, in fact it is the name of my grandmother and I use it as a sort of tribute, as she too represented the best of a generation now entirely lost to us.)

Ellen had been born in 1915. She lived alone in a large semi-detached house near Croydon. It was a good, safe, neighbourhood, what might once have been referred to as 'stockbroker belt'. Her husband had been a manager in the City during the days when that title meant something, and their home was evidence of the relative wealth and genuinely middle-class lifestyle they had enjoyed before he retired. He had died during the 1980s, leaving Ellen comfortable rather than well-off, but alone. Their daughter had emigrated and settled far away with her own family, so Ellen saw little of them and treasured the frequent phone calls across the seas as her only means of contact.

She had been active in local societies and groups for many years but, as she turned ninety, as is too often a spiteful fact of life, her brain was intact but her body started to fail. She suffered from mobility problems and had lost the sight in one eye. Despite the help provided by the authorities and her attentive neighbours, this well-spoken, intelligent lady became frail and unwittingly reclusive. It was too painful an effort for her even to move through the house. She became reliant on the meals on wheels service for food and spent much of the day sitting in her rocking chair just inside her front door, listening to Radio 4. She would sometimes stay there all night, it being easier just to pull a couple of nearby rugs over herself and to drift off in the chair, than steel herself for the short but excruciating journey to her downstairs bedroom.

Such an evening was 10 June 2009. She had fallen asleep in the chair some time after ten o'clock and so was oblivious to the Night Stalker as he broke the blades from a plastic vent fan set in her side kitchen window, giving him enough space to insert his arm through the circular hole in the glass and release the window catch. Nothing had been spent on the house for more than thirty years and so its security was virtually non-existent. It would have been a soft enough target for an inexperienced burglar; for Minstead man it was almost too easy. She had been awoken by him and, as she was to report to me later in a surprisingly strong voice, she had been very polite in telling him where the £20 or £30 in cash was when he asked, equally politely she assured me, where her money was.

The home help had arrived around eleven hours later, to find Ellen in her chair as usual but quite obviously distressed. The old lady had explained how she had used her panic alarm once the intruder had gone, but that nobody had come. Glossing over that deficiency in the system, the help had called the police and after local police had attended, the call was quickly passed on to the Minstead office and some of the team deployed. PC Tony Brooks mentioned it to me and pointed out that the victim was very old, very frail and although she was unhurt, there was an obvious risk that coping with the ordeal might prove difficult for her.

When I had instigated Minstead Lite I had anticipated such a situation: although nobody had yet died at the hands of the Night Stalker, there was always the risk, given the age group he was targeting, that somebody one day would. If there was any foreseeable chance of that then we would have to respond appropriately by suspending the Minstead Lite protocol – there could be some Minstead offences which needed an investigation akin to a homicide. What Tony told me made me think this might prove such a case and I grabbed my keys and phone and headed out to the scene. I wanted to be there to make sure we did everything that we ought to. For an hour or two the reviewer had to become a murder detective again.

Arriving in the neat, wide suburban street my first impression was of just how many people were flitting about near Ellen's house. Not just my team doing the house-to-house and the forensic staff working hard as usual, but neighbours, well-wishers stopping by to see how dear old Ellen was. My first question of a crime-scene examiner was whether in her judgement we ought to be maintaining the scene more carefully for investigation. She told me that entry and exit had been from the rear and so she was happy that we were doing no harm using the front path.

When I opened the front door, it was just a matter of two steps and I was there in front of Ellen. She was in the rocking chair, swathed in crocheted blankets despite the lunchtime June sunshine. She was talking to Debbie and Sam the FLOs, her strong tones and rounded vowels appearing quite incongruous to the context – as if the voice of a radio announcer had been dubbed on to this frail old body.

Sam saw me enter and said, 'Ooh, Ellen – this is Mr Sutton, he's the boss.'

I looked over and bowed my head slightly as I said, 'Hello.'

I saw this thin and wrinkled face flash into the most welcoming of smiles as she replied, 'Hello, Mr Sutton.'

'Oh, that's far too formal, Ellen. Please call me Colin.'

'Colin,' she said, pulling both of her hands out from under the blankets and using them to motion gently to me that I should get closer to her. As I did so she extended her right hand as if to shake mine. I took it, it was cold and about half the size of mine and, rather than just shaking it, she gripped and tugged me downwards. I let her do that, bending so my head was very close to hers. As it did, she brought her left hand over. I noticed that it still bore a very expensive-looking solitaire engagement ring and a wedding band – and I instantly thought she was lucky to have kept those from him.

Gripping my hand with both of hers as if she would never let go, she whispered in my ear, 'Colin. He interfered with me you know,' while looking me in the eye, her lips quivering but the words not faltering.

I wanted to cry, I wanted to shout out, I wanted to hug her. I recognised the euphemism as one typical of her generation. I had heard of elderly victims not revealing sexual assault because it was something their generation was so uncomfortable discussing. I knew that it had taken all her courage to tell me, that she had been keeping it to herself despite speaking to a dozen different people that morning.

This wonderful, resilient, educated and gentle old lady

had been reduced, in the twilight of her life, to explaining the most intimate loss of her dignity to a total stranger. I rarely felt emotion about the criminals I was chasing but at that very moment had the Night Stalker been there I would not have been able to restrain myself.

I told Ellen she was very brave, that we would look after her, and with a gentle squeeze of her hand went for a quick council of war with Sam and Debbie.

I was convinced Ellen needed to go to hospital but she had apparently already firmly declined that offer. The difficulty we had was that there just might have been forensic evidence to be found by a full examination, as is the usual practice with victims of sexual assault. But was she up to it? It is an intrusive and intimate procedure which inevitably adds to the victim's trauma but which is necessary if the assailant is to be prosecuted. How might it affect this most vulnerable of women? We agreed that the FLOs would broach the subject with her but that we would only push her if she were able to tell us more of the detail of her ordeal – and those details suggested it was likely that a full examination would yield useful evidence.

In the event, the forensic people told us pretty quickly that it looked like the Night Stalker had used his favourite screwdriver once more in gaining entry to the house and so we had a solid link to make it a Minstead offence. It was therefore not necessary to subject Ellen to a speculative search for DNA and she remained at home, medical services coming to visit her there, which at least spared her the upheaval of a stay in hospital.

I broke another of my personal rules in dealing with Ellen. In every one of the fifty or so murder investigations I led, I met with the victim's family, feeling it was only right for the bereaved to meet the man in charge of what was, for them, the most important investigation the police would ever conduct. I always did this with the family liaison officers present. However, I did not give the families my number and stressed to them that if they wanted to speak to me then that would of course be possible but it had to be arranged through the FLOs. The reasoning for this was twofold. First, the FLOs were trained and they had more time to dedicate to 'their' families than did I. Second, although it is human nature to want to contact the most senior person you are able to when there is an issue, if the families had direct access to me it would almost certainly lead to the FLOs being bypassed and effectively becoming redundant. I think most SIOs operated in this way and it was how the FLOs expected it to be.

However, perhaps because the case was so shocking, and because I knew that the initial liaison would have to be conducted with Ellen's daughter by phone rather than face to face, I agreed with Sam and Debbie that I would do it. The call was difficult to make but I found her daughter to be pragmatic and understanding. She would have found it very difficult to drop everything and return to the UK and I was in any case able to satisfy her that we were doing all we could for her mother. We agreed that we would keep in touch and I would call her as soon as I had any significant news.

The tragic postscript to all of this is that Ellen was so affected by what she had endured that, from the day of her attack forward, she barely ate a thing. Her aged body was in no state to cope with starvation and she deteriorated quickly, dying in hospital some seven weeks later. I broke the news to her daughter in another very difficult phone call. Not surprisingly, she took the view that the Night Stalker had killed Ellen – an assessment using logic against which I found it difficult to argue. Not that I wanted to, at all. I knew that he had killed her just as surely as if he had shot or strangled her on the night he broke into her home.

But although that was the common-sense conclusion, I knew it would not be one that any court would be able to reach. Had she died the following morning, or even after a day or two, then we might have had a chance. The intervening weeks, her virtual starvation and, crucially, the doctor's view in stating 'old age' on her death certificate meant that it would be impossible to prove causation. I explained this to her tearful and outraged daughter and promised to at least get a view from the Crown Prosecution Service, all the time knowing the answer I would get.

Ellen therefore was, officially, just another victim of a burglary and indecent assault but should forever be on the Night Stalker's conscience as a woman he killed. She will remain that in my thoughts.

Chapter 13

PLANNING PROACTIVITY – THE GROUNDWORK

I had been around divisions with burglary problems quite a few times; in the 1980s and 1990s it would have been hard to serve anywhere that did not suffer. And pretty frequently there would be a spate of burglaries which, by their method, told us we were very obviously looking at the work of one man. There was a standard response that, possibly surprisingly, was very often effective. You would identify the part of the division suffering most, cobble together a team of officers from here and there, sit them in vans and behind the curtains in friendly residents' bedrooms, and wait for him to come along and commit a crime before your very eyes.

The principle was very well tried and tested and, indeed, was what had been attempted by the Minstead team in the past. I had to consider why it had failed; what were the differences with the Night Stalker? Well, first and most obvious was the size of the area of his offending. When this is just an estate or a part of a division it is perfectly possible to mount a comprehensive observation with a group of ten or twenty officers. But Minstead offences were much more widely spread; effectively his patch was one quarter of Greater London. As if that was not enough, it was clear that, whatever his motivation, the Night Stalker was much more cunning and aware than your average burglar desperate to crash a door to steal enough for his next fix. The preparation, his patience, the detail and regularity of his methods, and the uniformity of the type of property and victim he attacked all pointed to a man who took care – pride, almost – in what he did. One manifestation of this was his forensic awareness. He was careless – uncaring even – about leaving his DNA at scenes but never ever left a fingerprint. It was generally accepted that the likely explanation for this was that he knew we had his prints on file, from earlier convictions, but that he also knew his DNA was not on the database and so no matter how much he left it would not lead us to him. So thoughtful a criminal would only be caught by similarly cunning and meticulous action on our part.

I knew that both of these difficulties could be addressed but was aware that it would cost in terms of officers and resources in a way that would only be possible with support from the very highest levels of the Met. There was no way at all that we could mount an operation with any chance of success using only what we had. I was going to have to go begging and back it up with a firm and credible plan.

My first step would have to be establishing where to look. The Night Stalker's immutable preference for 1930s properties was useful as this would help narrow down the individual streets at risk but, since what I envisaged was essentially a visual containment of an area, it was obvious that that area had to be smaller than all of south-east London. I would be fortunate to get a hundred officers and so needed to focus. My first stop, therefore, was the analyst Richard Moore, to see if he could suggest a suitable and containable area from a spot of crime-pattern analysis. But it was not quite as simple as asking him. This was where the screening policy was likely to cause issues – for Richard's Minstead records would just include the offences which had been adopted for investigation by the team. How confident could we be that the pattern produced by looking at them would accurately reflect the locations where the Night Stalker was most likely to strike? What I wanted – needed – was an analysis of all the possible Minstead offences.

We knew from the Farnaby Road offence that the old screening process was not absolutely reliable and so I wanted everything ruled in, if only to see if that produced a result substantially different from that when only 'taken' offences were analysed. I appreciated this would involve a considerable amount of fiddly research and work on his part, so it was with a degree of trepidation that I entered Richard's office to make the request.

'Richard, you probably aren't going to like this, but I need you to do something important but not easy for me...'

He looked up at me with the sort of mixture of intrigue and horror that you would expect such a statement to inspire. 'Go on, what's that?'

'Well, I want some analysis done and a crime-pattern map drawn up, but I want it to include all the offences that have been reported to us as possible Minstead offences...'

Richard narrowed his eyes and began to frown. I was not sure if he was going to explode with anger or burst into tears.

'Not just those for which we have taken responsibility to

investigate,' I continued. I thought I might as well make the impossible request absolutely clear before I sent the poor man home on sick leave.

Richard steadied his gaze on me for a few seconds without speaking. Able to contain himself no more, a huge beam spread across his face and, chuckling first, he reached down to his left, saying, 'What, like this?' and producing a weighty sheaf of paper from his desk drawer.

I was bewildered for a moment, then I realised his horror had just been an act – a very convincing one. As he placed the paper pile in front of me I realised what it was.

'You've already done it? What… how d-did you know…?' I was gibbering, stammering, genuinely shocked. How could he have known I would ask for it?

'Truth is, there are a few of us who were never really happy with the screening process. We worried that it would skew the analysis and so I've been running this report alongside the official one for some time now. It isn't in truth a lot different…'

But it will add so much weight, just in sheer numbers, to what I need to prove.'

'What, are we going proactive then, Colin?'

'Well, I hope so, if I can persuade the great and the good at the Yard.'

'About bloody time.'

I could have hugged Richard there and then. Not just because I had in my hand a document that was going to be crucial to my plans and which I had thought would take days or weeks to arrive. Almost more important was the realisation that he and others were obviously going to be with me in trying to change the direction of the team. I was going to need support from below and above; if the team were likely to be on board, then that was half the battle.

Next stop was Nathan's office. I was like a child with a new bike on Christmas morning, I just could not wait to share the good news with my DI. He was just as impressed with the attitude and initiative shown by Richard Moore and expressed his absolute support for what I was trying to achieve. With the cynicism unfortunately too often justifiably found among police officers, he expressed his doubts that I would find the top brass as accommodating.

'If they cared about this then we would have had more people for the last four years,' was his entirely reasonable assessment.

He then made a statement that I had heard from others – and with which I found it very difficult to argue:

'You know, if the victims of this were aged between eighteen and thirty-six instead of sixty-three and ninety-six there'd have been such an outcry in the press, such a determination within the job, that it would have been sorted years ago. But it's just a load of old ladies, not sexy enough for people to get outraged, is it?'

'We care, Nathan. I care. I am outraged.'

'Are we enough though?'

'We can be. And just think how sweet that will make it when we succeed.'

Chapter 14

THE ATMs

Thomas was eighty-eight years old. He had come to the UK as a refugee at the start of the Second World War, during which his linguistic skills had meant he was a valuable member of the code-breaking team at Bletchley Park. He lived alone in his 1930s bay-fronted semi in Ingram Road, a quiet residential street in Thornton Heath. The outside of his house had been virtually untouched for decades and was another which shouted the age of its occupier. Classic Minstead country, both by geography and architecture. So much so, as we were to discover, that he had been attacked by the Night Stalker twice.

The first time, on 30 May 2009, the burglary and theft of some loose change was left with the local division to investigate. The reasoning for this seems to have been that our suspect never attacked men – which of course we know was not true. Rarely, yes, but not never. As such it was not really a justification for not assuming the investigation and is another example of using 'criteria' to try to control the number of cases piling up and increasing Minstead's workload.

In the first two hours of 13 August that same year, the Night Stalker paid Thomas a return visit. This time he was not so lucky: the Night Stalker hit the jackpot. He found Thomas's nest egg of around £3,000 in cash, hidden in the bottom of a wardrobe, and also took his bank card. That was not all Thomas lost that night – due to being forced to take part in an act of mutual masturbation, the Night Stalker also took his pride.

By the time of the second burglary Minstead Lite was in operation; there was no question that we would not have taken it on, even if Thomas had not told us how he had wryly remarked to the intruder, 'Hello, oh, it's you again.'

Not that we had them, but any doubts that the offender was the Night Stalker would be firmly dispelled just a couple of hours later. Three attempts had been made to withdraw cash using Thomas's bank card at an external ATM at Gogi's Off-Licence in Honor Oak Park, SE23. Each of these had failed as the wrong pin number had been entered; the spirited old man had ignored the threats and given his attacker a false PIN. He told us that he had figured that by the time the Night Stalker found out he had misled him the police would be there and he would be safe.

I was called by Nathan Eason and advised of these developments by phone as I was on my daily slog through the M25 rush hour to Lewisham. Not only did he explain what had happened but also mentioned something of which I had no knowledge at all – that this particular cash machine was seemingly a favourite of the Night Stalker's, he having used it before on a couple of occasions. He reasoned, quite correctly in my view, that the location of the attempts was very persuasive of the theory that it had been our man. But there was more. The last time the machine had been used by the Night Stalker, more than two years ago, had resulted in his stealing £300 from it.

Simon Morgan had then arranged for the Met Technical Support Unit to provide covert CCTV cameras to be installed near the ATM in case our suspect returned. As well as being buoyed by this, I was also a tiny bit peeved not to have been told about it before. That I had been kept in the dark about a potentially significant line of enquiry was frustrating and naturally made me wonder what else might have been kept in the dark, but this was soon forgotten when I imagined how the morning might pan out. By the time I arrived at the office the Technical Support Unit would have retrieved and delivered the footage. We were going to get a look at the Night Stalker.

As I strode hopefully into the sergeants' office where I guessed Neville Hylton and Adam Spiers would be studying the frames, I immediately sensed the mood. And it was palpably flat, Adam thumbing through his mobile for a number and Neville munching on his daily morning bowl of granola.

'So, come on then, what's he look like?' I eagerly prompted.

Both looked up, at each other and then as Adam rolled his eyes, Neville responded, 'Like any other bloke in a cagoule zipped up to his nose with the hood pulled over his face.'

Hence the general mood. Neville turned his PC monitor slightly as I joined him behind the desk and after a couple of weary mouse clicks, I could see for myself. Objectively, the footage from the camera with the widest shot of the scene was very good, particularly considering it had been at night – not too grainy and even displaying colours well. It was easy to watch, at 3.51 am as a medium-height, medium-build man in a mid-blue cagoule and dark trousers walked briskly from Lessing Street, making a couple of 'lifesaver' glances behind and breaking into a trot as he traversed the zebra crossing towards the north side of Honor Oak Park. But to glean any descriptive details of him – his age, his build, even his ethnicity – was impossible. It really could have been any of the many thousands of adult men in south London.

The footage from the camera placed closer to the ATM was not much better. The sum total of our new knowledge was that the Night Stalker possessed a blue cagoule, black trousers and white trainers. And that he was very, very careful to conceal his identity, even to the point of still wearing a face-covering, when trying to use a stolen debit card.

Inside I felt just as disappointed as my colleagues. The exuberant hope that had made the drudge of my commute so bearable that morning was replaced by the sinking realisation that it was not going to be that easy. How madly optimistic must I have been to imagine that it might be? Trying hard to hide my disappointment, and very aware that my role as always was to inspire not depress, I suggested that we got Nathan in and that the four of us review all the footage and have a sort of brainstorming session to see what else we might be able to glean from the footage.

Each of us grabbed a coffee, pulled up a chair and sat there, pens poised, with our red notebooks. Neville operated the pause and rewind as we went through it, frame by frame, bouncing ideas, remarking on the tiniest feature and frequently bemoaning the Night Stalker's luck. And just as often, our lack of it. When we had finished we were a little more optimistic that despite the heavy disguise of his person there were a few things we might take forward.

Uppermost was the route he had walked to and from the cash machine. He had approached on foot from Lessing Street, turning left to head east on Honor Oak Park and crossing the road towards Gogi's. After his abortive efforts to get his hands on yet more of poor Thomas's money, he had immediately crossed Honor Oak Park again but instead of returning the way he had come he could be seen to walk off south, down Ballina Street, looking west the next street down from and parallel to Lessing Street.

Applying the tradecraft of the street while using the technology of Google Street View, we hypothesised. Say he had left a car near the top end of Lessing Street, then to approach it from a different direction after using the card (so as to reduce suspicion) he might use the alley we could see at the rear of the shops in Honor Oak Park, which connected Ballina Street with Lessing Street. The footage did not show far enough into Ballina Street to be sure, but he did appear to cross the road towards the alley just before he disappeared out of the top of the frame.

Nathan and I pretty much immediately went down to Honor Oak Park, asking Neville and Adam to round up as many of the team as they could before they all joined us. We found that the alley between Ballina and Lessing Streets gave access not only to the rear of the shops but, by steep iron fire-escape staircases, also to the flats above them. Did anyone living in them see or hear anything? Did they have any additional CCTV that might help track our man further? We scoped the house-to-house enquiries we would need to make and called Adam just to make sure the troops were on their way. And in the meantime, leading from the front, we shrugged our shoulders and made a start.

When the rest of the team turned up Nathan corralled the eight or so detectives at one end of the alley and briefed them. I noticed then that the side of the alley away from the rear of the shops was bordered by a thick privet hedge. Which might very well be a good place to discard a stolen debit card to which you had an incorrect PIN, I mused. Continuing on that train of thought I looked at the many refuse bins behind the shops and also at the drains in the alley. I swiftly concluded I would call and ask for a POLSA – a team of uniform officers specially trained and equipped to conduct widespread searches. If we could just find that card, then perhaps we would get DNA to confirm absolutely it was the Night Stalker – or even a fingerprint which might lead us to his identity? The possibilities were real, even if history told us the likelihood was low. I made the call and, unusually, a team was immediately available; they promised to arrive at the scene within two hours.

I looked down to the end of the alley and saw Nathan had finished his briefing; the detectives were fanning out with their clipboards to knock on doors and he was now glued to his mobile phone, pacing wide circles as he spoke. When he finished the call he came briskly over to me, motioning to the phone theatrically as he thrust it into his jacket pocket. He began to address me as we were still walking towards each other, reducing the volume of his voice as we got closer.

'That was Mr Morgan. He says he doesn't want us making a big fuss here, that it will create fear in the community if it looks like a big thing has gone on.'

I mouthed '*What the fuck?*' and considered my reply, walking closer to Nathan while checking carefully that none of the team was near enough to hear what I was planning to say.

'Possibly a bit late for that, given we've got ten of us banging on doors?'

'He said we should keep it low key…'

'Well if house-to-house isn't low key enough, Christ knows what he'll think when the POLSA team gets here. They don't really do low key.'

'Funnily enough, I mentioned that we might do a search and he specifically said not to get a POLSA team.'

'Too late. I've already ordered them…'

'Shit, well, you'd better cancel them.'

I thought about it for half a second and decided that if I was ever going to make an impact on the investigation I'd been saddled with, then I had to make a stand.

'Nathan, look, it is all on me. If there is a problem I will make sure that he knows you passed on the message – and that I ignored it. Quite frankly, I think that it's worth risking a bit of angst in the community for the chance of getting some evidence. I'm going to leave them running.'

That Nathan simply replied with a mumbled 'Fair enough', that he did not try to persuade me otherwise, told me he at least was not opposed to what I planned.

An hour or so later I briefed the POLSA Inspector, as usual signing a written note of the parameters for the search and its objectives before his team began. I left them to get on with their work and pitched in again helping out with the house-to-house enquiries. It was increasingly likely that nobody had seen anything and that there was no new CCTV to be found. Then my phone rang. I saw from the display that it was Nathan, so instead of answering I stepped around the corner into the alley and waved at him. The phone went silent and he strode briskly towards me.

'Guess what? They've found a debit card in the hedge.'

'Excellent,' I almost screamed, eyes wide open, hoping that we had not only gained a potential breakthrough but also that my firm stance would be vindicated.

'Not exactly, no. But it is relevant…' My DI looked me straight in the eye and took a deep breath. 'It *is* a card belonging to a Minstead victim, but *not* last night's. It's from the last time he used this ATM, from an offence in Dulwich in November 2007. The one where he got three hundred quid out of Gogi's with it.'

I looked at the green-and-white Lloyds TSB card sealed in an evidence bag. I wondered how much two years exposed to the elements in a London privet might have degraded any trace evidence it might once have borne. I wondered also how it could be that such a potentially valuable piece of evidence could have been missed at the time it had been stolen. Then I realised it was most likely that the truth was, no search had been conducted back then, presumably so as not to upset or alarm the local community. Finally, I wondered what other interesting twists and turns this investigation had up its sleeve for me and whether I ought to just accept it or shout out.

The August ATM enquiry didn't really take us any further – Thomas's card was never found and there was no trace of DNA or fingerprints on the card from 2007. Nevertheless, it became clear that the Night Stalker was evolving his methods; like any business he had to move with the times or be left behind. So many of his potential victims had begun to use debit cards rather than cash – probably due to state pension payments now being made by bank transfer rather than by cash at the post office – that his focus was likely increasingly to be on stealing plastic and hoping he could extract the PINs by instilling fear.

Within a few days he had again stolen a debit card from a burglary in Bromley and tried to withdraw cash with it from a different ATM. This time there was a shockingly brazen irony to his effort. The cash machine was located on the wall of an HSBC Bank branch, at the time standing on the corner of Westmoreland Road and Pickhurst Lane, halfway between Bromley and West Wickham. The community-spirited staff there had willingly tried to assist the Minstead investigation by displaying an official Met appeal for information poster in their front window – a window immediately next to the external ATM. One imagines they chose this location for maximum impact, its bold colours and striking suggested-image of the suspect easily drawing the attention of those using the cash facility. Thus was it that as he was trying to extract some cash from his latest victim's account, the Night Stalker cannot have helped but see the e-fit – his own e-fit – and details of some of his awful crimes, staring at him just a couple of feet away.

We made the expected enquires local to the bank. CCTV from a nearby Esso filling station showed that the only movement close to the time of the ATM attempt was one car with a solitary driver passing it towards the bank. The quality of the images was good enough to identify the make and model of the car easily, even for the non-expert. It was plainly a Peugeot 406 saloon, in silver. The sort of car used at the time by hundreds of minicab drivers in suburban London.

For what was the first, but would prove not to be the last, time in this investigation, I shied away from repeating my 'chasing cars' experience of the Bellfield investigation some five years previously. The suspicion around the car simply wasn't strong enough, in my judgement, to justify a change of course to a line of enquiry which would have sucked in almost the entire team. We raised an action for the intelligence team to see if any man on the suspect list had associations with such a car and I ensured the team were briefed on its appearance so they could bear it in mind. Beyond that I was reluctant to go all in on the car – principally because we had absolutely no proof that the Night Stalker had been inside it.

A further ATM attempt, back in Honor Oak but this time at the post office on Brockley Rise, confirmed that these machines might prove a fruitful line of enquiry for us. Given that Gogi's was still his clear favourite, that one had to be the priority. We had put the cameras in – what more could we do? I made my view clear to Nathan and Neville – we had enough unrecognisable pictures of the Night Stalker, we certainly didn't need any more. What would work though was if we could somehow organise ourselves with the ability to detain him there the next time he turned up. We were united in the firm opinion that it would be when rather than if. A rather fanciful and somewhat Heath Robinson-esque discussion arose as to how we could get some sort of trap built to contain him. As ridiculous as that sounds – and it really was, quite ridiculous – it was useful in that it did lead to a wider discussion and our hatching a plan to ask the major banks if they could restrict the use of debit cards for the elderly in south-east London between midnight and 7am.

By October 2009, I had been formally appointed as Senior Investigating Officer after Simon Morgan's hospitalisation. From that point I had a lot more freedom to be creative in trying to progress the ATM plan but also in my longer-term desire to see the operation move to a more proactive strategy. As a stopgap measure, before the move to full proactivity could be planned, resourced and executed, I decided to put human surveillance on Gogi's ATM. This was relatively easy to do as the neighbouring shop was a minicab office, which meant stationary cars with occupants were a common sight nearby, especially across the road in Ballina Street – from where there was a perfect view of the ATM. As I had sensed was increasingly the case, the team relished the prospect of doing something positive to catch our target and there was no shortage of volunteers to crew-up a surveillance car. Most nights either Neville or Adam would be in charge; I left it to their judgement as to whether somebody using Gogi's cash machine should be pounced on there and then or followed and stopped elsewhere. The latter would be tactically preferable as it would not disclose what we were doing – but if they were sure he was a good suspect then the priority would be to leave him no room to escape. The observation would commence each night at midnight and cease at 5.30 am – my thinking being that they were very generous parameters since the earliest time he had recently used an ATM was 2 am and the latest 4.15 am.

Four or five nights into the surveillance, at midnight on Saturday, 17 October 2009, as the watching officers got into position in Ballina Street, the Night Stalker was already in the home of an 82-year-old woman in Lee. While they observed a steady stream of young revellers and urban foxes moving up and down Honor Oak Park, he was spending more than four hours with his latest victim, chatting, threatening and eventually leaving her physically unscathed but having taken all the cash she had to hand and her debit card – to which she had, in sheer terror, given him what she believed was the correct PIN.

By the time their shift came to its end, Neville Hylton and his team of two others were ready for bed. Six hours in a car concentrating and trying to remain unseen is mentally tough. That they had shown the utmost conscientiousness by remaining at their post a little beyond their allotted time did not surprise me, and it was a fact that I could happily demonstrate by producing the footage from the hidden cameras. The police car with the Minstead team could be seen gently pulling away at exactly 5.36 am, another unsuccessful tour of duty watching and waiting was over.

When, some five hours later, I arrived at Lewisham to be told that not only had we had another offence overnight but that he had used the victim's card to withdraw cash at Gogi's I experienced a rush of different emotions. Disappointment, anger, incredulity – none of them was a good feeling. It took an hour or so to get the footage downloaded and there it was. Yes, the team had left at 5.36 am, just seven minutes before 5.43 am, when the Night Stalker appeared on the cameras, and eight before he was making his illicit withdrawal a minute later. They had missed him by the narrowest of margins.

I was never one for recriminations, and in truth none was justified in this instance. It is often the case with police officers that one's greatest critic is oneself – and that was where I turned my attention. But as I wrestled with depressed introspection, I needed to be realistic. I had set the parameters, generously, based on the current and latest intelligence we had. The team had carried out my instructions absolutely to the letter. Nobody was to blame; once again he simply had all the luck and we had none of it. But that did not stop me from beating myself up that I should have made the time slots longer, nor them fretting that they should have just given it another twenty minutes until first light.

Such self-doubt is often inevitable when there is such a close call with success – if we did not care about what we were doing we would never succeed at anything. You are always dealing with 'what ifs' and 'if onlys' in the immediate aftermath of close failure. But the pain it caused to all of us was never really soothed until we finally arrested him. And when we did, those pictures of him from the near miss in a grey top with a black stripe over the arms, as well as those of the blue cagoule from his previous appearance at Gogi's in August, were to become very important.

Chapter 15

PLANNING PROACTIVITY – THE MEETINGS

The offences had been coming in steadily during September, sixteen reports in nineteen days. Now with a free hand as the SIO it was possible for me to put the proactive plan into action. The theory of what I intended to do was essentially quite simple.

When I was a young PC at Tottenham I had played a very small role when, in the early 1980s, we had successfully captured two lone serial criminals simply by observations across the area in which they were offending so prolifically. Steven Prendergast, known as 'The Haringey Rapist', and Errol Dobson, dubbed 'The Louvre Burglar', found their respective sprees brought to a conclusion when they committed offences before the very eyes of officers. But, being both unsophisticated and over-confident, they had simply not noticed the officers sitting observing them from houses, cars and vans. And their offending had been confined to a relatively small area, just a few streets really, which made visual containment of it easy using just twenty or so officers. That was the sort of number you could conjure up quite easily on a division by borrowing a few from here and there and perhaps a few from your close neighbours. But what if you were trying to lockdown a much bigger area? That was the immediate difficulty, but there were others too.

The basic tactic I wanted to use was sound but every indication we had was that the Night Stalker was careful, cunning and very aware of his surroundings. The simple type of primarily vehicle-based observation had been tried before on several occasions over the years, most recently in Farnaby Road. Yet it had always failed despite being in the streets where he was regularly operating. Who knew if he had walked past the covert officers, spotted them and walked on? We had no way of telling and so had to eliminate that possibility from the plan.

In West Yorkshire Police in the 1990s I had been Head of Force Intelligence, which meant I had overall responsibility for the surveillance teams and the technical support unit that used all manner of bugs and cameras to facilitate observing criminals. I learned there, from some hugely experienced and skilled officers, that the only way to do surveillance and guarantee not to be found out was to be completely invisible. '*They can't know we are there and they can't know we have been there*' was the mantra. To do that ten years later across a huge swathe of London I was going to need help. Quite a lot of it.

The geographic dimension was incredibly daunting, so much so that more than once I was on the point of concluding it just couldn't be done. Rather than keeping to a few streets like Prendergast and Dobson, the Night Stalker had a much wider theatre of operations. It consisted, essentially, of an entire quarter of Greater London, virtually from the south bank of the Thames round anti-clockwise to the A23. To observe all of that was obviously quite impossible; we needed to focus our efforts on somewhere a little more manageable. Well, considerably so really.

Using Richard Moore's comprehensive analysis package, which took account of every possible Minstead offence, it became clear that the most likely area for an observation was the favourite hunting ground around the A232 at Shirley, to the east of Croydon. Indeed, so prolific had he been around that location that a (albeit rather wide) perimeter could be drawn in which almost one out of every three Minstead offences had occurred. To cover that comprehensively I knew it would need a lot of officers – I estimated (rather conservatively in the event) that it might be around a hundred. I could cobble together fewer than twenty from the team, so it was obvious from the start that we would require a great deal of help from many other teams. I would need them willingly to provide people, vehicles, communications kit and other equipment if a surveillance operation were to have any chance of beginning, let alone succeeding.

I booked a meeting room at Scotland Yard and crafted an email, as concise as was possible to make sure it got read, but still with enough detail to convey the seriousness of the offences, the rate of offending and the need to do something about it, quickly. This I sent to a dozen or so leaders at the squads and branches I thought might have sufficient resilience in their teams to be able to help, inviting them to sit with me around a table to discuss it. What I did not expect was that when the meeting convened, there were more than twenty officers around the table. It was just so heartening to realise that the Minstead case had got under their skin to the extent that some had invited others I had not thought of. And they delivered, offering help both in resources but also expertise that I had not dare dream of.

As the discussions went on it was obvious that these people wanted to help, they had a wealth of experience and creativity. They were fully bought-in to the concept of completely unseen control of the area. It was an absolute pleasure to see such capable people taking ownership of the problem. For the first time I realised that other people really did care about Minstead.

Soon a detailed plan had evolved. We knew from the Farnaby Road CCTV footage that the Night Stalker walked to the home he wanted to attack, at least for the last part of his route. We knew from Farnaby Road that he probably did not use public transport and, given the wide area in which he operated, must therefore have used a vehicle. We had never seen it though, presumably due to his not wanting to leave an identifiable car or van close by while he was busy burgling. The area we were to target was largely residential, good-class private dwellings with very little pedestrian traffic after dark. And the demographics of the locality were such that very few of the occasional passers-by were black. So, by observing every inch of the pavement in the observed roads we could control them. Nobody would be able to walk in or out without us seeing them. If we were patient and he had no idea we were there, the Night Stalker would eventually come to offend right under our noses. It would take discipline and patience, but the consensus was that it was possible.

The operation would have no officers sitting in cars or

walking about the 'plot'. Everyone would be inside a building. If it were not possible to see some part of the street unaided then the technical support unit would install hidden cameras to fill in the gaps. There would be a mobile surveillance team on stand-by outside the plot but close to it, so that if a suspect needed to be questioned, he could be followed at a significant distance and would be well away from the area before officers stopped him. This was of the utmost importance: the last thing we needed was word getting around on the street that there was surveillance going on in Shirley. Although we didn't know who the Night Stalker was, it was a reasonable assumption that he would be well-connected to the local criminal fraternity and likely get to hear of any leak. The whole thing would be covered where possible by air support too, at an altitude whereby its presence was undetectable on the ground; although given the time of year I was fearful that cloud and bad weather would too often hamper their efforts it was potentially a good safety net. Lastly, and possibly most surprisingly, we would have use of a control room at 'Central 3000', a windowless complex at the centre of an anonymous office block near Vauxhall usually reserved for ongoing kidnaps, terrorism or similar fast-moving and very serious cases. This would be a great help – as well as the usual computers and radio equipment it had a bank of eighteen TV screens across one wall, into which the feed from any of thousands of local authority or Transport for London CCTV cameras could be piped and recorded. As well, of course, as images from the hidden cameras we might have ourselves placed.

It was certainly going to be a grand production: in total we came up with a requirement for roughly one hundred and fifty officers. Once the sums had been done it deflated the mood somewhat. I had no experience of making a request to the Force Tasking Group – the body that, ultimately, would have to agree to this huge use of resources – but one of my colleagues at our meeting who was a frequent bidder there confided, 'I honestly don't think you have a hope of that. In truth you will be lucky to get half of it – only then if you make a really good case and present it well. It's two deputy assistant commissioners who decide, they can't be had over.'

A quick reassessment was then done. Looking at the map and relating it to the crime-pattern analysis showed that if we restricted the plot to north of the A232 and slimmed it slightly, it could probably be controlled by around seventy officers. Which, I was assured by those who knew, was still a bit of an ask but much more likely to be met with approval; there would be no chance of significantly more. This redrawing of our boundaries still gave us an area where one in six offences had taken place, so despite the odds being halved I maintained my optimism that it would succeed, accepting that it might mean a little more patience. Now all that was needed was to get the go-ahead from the bosses.

Sometimes, a difficulty with having so many capable people trying to help you is that, just now and then, they will set wheels in motion which in truth you would rather they had asked you about first. This was about to become very clear to me.

I was only too aware that in the coming days I had to put my bid to the Force Tasking Group together. I had the basics in mind and a load of notes and mind-maps from the initial planning meeting, but needed to find two or three hours to fine-tune them and weave them together into that killer, irresistible PowerPoint which would seal the deal. But finding the time to do so at Lewisham was proving impossible – there was just so much going on and I was pulling ten-hour days with ninety minutes travelling each side. It would have to wait until the weekend when I could sit down in the relative calm of my own living room and be creative.

Unbeknown to me though, a colleague from the meeting had given notice to the Tasking Group and so just two days after the planning meeting I received a call on my mobile, while I was at Lewisham engrossed in discussing some exhibit submissions with Neville and Nathan.

'Hello, Mr Sutton, this is Inspector Adler, I work in planning and events at Scotland Yard.'

'Oh, hello…'

'Yes, I have managed to squeeze your application into our Force Tasking Group meeting today, you have got the eleven o'clock slot.'

I instinctively looked at my watch; it was 9.35 am.

'Well, that's very good of you Inspector, thank you – but I really am a bit too busy to do it today. Could you put me back until next week, please?'

'No, actually I can't. We are fully booked up now until the first week in November. It is either today or in six weeks' time I am afraid.'

Up to that point it was a cordial if businesslike conversation. But his next remark grated, making me possibly uncharacteristically angry.

'Of course, if it really isn't that urgent or important then I can tell the DACs that you aren't that bothered to come today…'

'It isn't a question of bothered, it's just that I am too bloody busy!' I raised my tone, betraying my annoyance.

'Well, we are all very busy these days—'

I cut across him, quite rudely really but still not wishing to start an ultimately pointless discussion comparing the relative difficulties involved in leading major investigations with those of organising meetings, but nevertheless furious and trying desperately to control my anger.

'Fine, OK, I will be there.'

After the call Neville and Nathan were silent, waiting for me to explain what had gone on, having only heard my side of the conversation but discerning my annoyance.

'I need to get to the Yard by eleven for the tasking meeting. Can one of you give me a lift so I can think on the way?'

By the time I was dropped off in Broadway by the iconic revolving sign it was 10.35. I had the most important presentation of my career coming up in less than half an hour, armed only with two sheets of A4 notes, the handwriting spidery and barely legible due to the frequent intervention of London potholes and speed bumps. Then, as I approached the entrance vestibule – disaster! I felt on my chest for the lanyard to swipe my way through the barriers into the Yard and realised that, in the rush to get on the road quickly, I had left my warrant card on my desk. If I tried to negotiate with the security staff for entry without it I knew the process would be so lengthy that I would be likely to miss next week's meeting let alone the one going on upstairs now. Panic. Think logically, Colin. I saw Neville and the VW Golf disappearing out of sight towards Victoria Street and hurriedly jabbed his speed dial on my old Nokia. For once luck was with me and he answered straight away; a three-minute trip round the block brought him back to me. I borrowed his card, got through the barriers and up in the lift. I hung his identification around my neck being careful to ensure that Neville's photograph was unseen – we looked absolutely nothing like each other.

When the sneery Inspector Adler showed me to a seat to wait for my slot I had about ten minutes to breathe deeply and compose myself.

I was shown into the room, about ten rows of chairs set facing a desk behind which were the deputy assistant commissioners, Lynne Owens and Sue Akers. Lynne had been a colleague of my wife Louise at Surrey and Sue was the Child Protection DI at Islington during my time there in the same rank in the main CID office, which meant I knew them both, not well but certainly on nodding acquaintance terms. A uniform chief inspector from a Borough was just finishing off his request for assistance with a vehicle-crime initiative, walking the meeting through a smart-looking, vibrant PowerPoint presentation with impressive charts, graphs and photographs of cars with smashed windows. Inspector Adler sidled up to me and whispered, 'Can I have your presentation please, sir?'

I looked down at the two sheets of scrawl and, despite the agony of my predicament had to chuckle.

'No, I need it,' I replied, directing his gaze to my notes with my eyes.

'I mean your memory stick, or CD.'

'Yes, I knew that. I don't have one, just these.'

The nod he gave me with pursed lips was difficult to read. I would like to think that he felt great sympathy for me, but on reflection it was more likely he was worried that I was quite mad – and possibly slightly dangerous. Just another chancer of a detective, trying to busk it in his ordered administrative world.

Slick PowerPoint Chief Inspector had finished and naturally he had been given everything he had asked for. Inspector Adler called out, 'DCI Sutton, Operation Minstead.'

His tone still failed miserably to supress his disdain, and I had that horrible feeling of vulnerability you get when you stand up or ask a question in a crowded room and everyone cranes to look at you. I picked my way carefully between the closely set chairs and made my way over to the lectern with the computer controls. Which of course I had not the slightest need whatsoever to use. As I did so DAC Lynne Owens smiled and asked me how I was; DAC Sue Akers said it was nice to see me, both called me Colin. They were being friendly; Inspector Adler looked crestfallen.

I began my pitch. I explained right at the start the huge resources I was seeking and what we wanted to do with them, then going on to try to justify it I gave a short history of Operation Minstead. I ploughed through the statistics and numbers I had scribbled on my journey, how many known offences, the number of suspected offences, the upturn in the rate of attacks in the last year. Every now and then I had real difficulty in making out my own handwriting, so badly had the rush and the jolting disturbed me. It was terse, dry stuff. I was fearful that the eyes of everybody present were glazing over, there seemed to be no reaction from anybody except Inspector Adler, who suddenly seemed to have regained some of his joviality.

I was dying on my feet and I knew it. I had no option but to carry on, I thought, but when I saw a flicker of interest after I pointed out that the victims were all aged between sixty-eight and ninety-six, an idea came to me. Now I really was busking it. I set my notes down on the lectern and looked directly at the two senior officers on whose support my whole plan depended.

'The bottom line, really, is this. We've got an 80-year-old woman needing an HIV test. I've got a man who was a hero of Bletchley Park who's too scared to tell our family liaison officer what this man did to him. I've got a 96-year-old half-blind woman clutching my arm and confiding in a thin, pleading voice that "He interfered with me". This has got to stop and it's on all of us. All of us need to take responsibility for stopping it as soon as we can. And this plan is the best shot we have at it, the best way to change the narrative from chasing him to lying in wait for him.'

Everyone was looking now, even Inspector Adler. The DACs looked at each other for a moment, both smiled and turned to me in unison.

'You are pushing on an open door, Colin,' said Lynne Owens as Sue Akers looked down at her papers, drawing a tick or something as she simply announced, 'Approved.'

We were going proactive.

Chapter 16

THE FIRST NIGHT OF SURVEILLANCE

The arrangements took a few weeks to get put into place. In the meantime, while I was visiting Central 3000 for the first time to be led, agog, around its wonderful facilities, officers from my team and those coming over to help were busy finding observation posts, putting together briefings and working out who was going to do what. The operational details took a few days to work out and refine, and in some ways, given the scale of the undertaking, it is remarkable that they were completed as quickly as they were.

Wednesday, 28 October 2009 was to be the first day of surveillance. Having done my day job, as it were, and gone home for dinner, a shower and a change of clothes, I battled back through late rush-hour traffic on the M25 to return to Lewisham by 8 pm; the briefing was set to start at 9 – it would, I hoped, be 9.30 thereafter, but I had added an extra half an hour to the first day so there would be time to iron out any last-minute creases.

I sat at my desk in the unusually quiet major incident suite, knowing without doubt that this was to be the most important briefing I would ever give. I had been supervising and leading police officers for many years, I had stood in front of a group of officers to give them information and instructions literally thousands of times – but somehow this was different. It was not the subject matter. As serious as Minstead was, there had been those with lives at immediate risk, firearms operations – briefings of the most momentous consequences – in the past which had never felt the same. My heart was racing, my mouth was dry and as I scanned my notes the bubbles in the mind-map I had drawn seemed to dance like some cruel video game. This was, I concluded, because it was just so vital that what we were about to commence was done properly. One slip, one giveaway chink of light from a curtain, one piece of paper dropped in the street… That's all it would take for the ever-vigilant Night Stalker to realise all was not normal, to abort his wicked mission and slip back into the darkness. I found myself thinking of how I should play it, how I ought to write down almost exactly what I was going to say. I turned to a clean page in my red book and began writing.

I got as far as the full stop after 'Good evening ladies and gentlemen, thank you for coming.' I stopped and stared at the sentence, at the book, and asked myself another question:

'What the bloody hell are you doing?'

There I was, the longest-serving senior investigating officer in the Met. I had been leading major investigations for fourteen years, I had been supervising, briefing and leading police officers for twenty-six. I'd never read a script; I'd always relied just on a few notes and trusted my ability to speak to them in an engaging and human way. And here I was writing a speech like a nervous best man the day after the stag night. I had always got by, always succeeded in the past by knowing what I wanted, knowing what had to be done, making it clear to the team and trusting them to then get on with it. Why should this be any different? It was no time to change the way I did things now. The last thing this team needed was a stumbling, monotone prepared script. I just had to be me, to trust myself and do it the way I always had. Ripping the page from the book with a degree of self-disgust, I turned back to the page of skeleton notes and strode out towards the briefing room.

Although the briefing/meeting room at Lewisham was unusually large, so, this time, was the team. By just before 9 pm so many were standing around the edges, the thirty or so seats having been taken up by the early arrivals, that I several times informally invited them to sit on the desks, secretly pleased that enough of them were still disciplined enough not to do so until it was okayed by the senior officer. Not for my own aggrandisement – I had been called 'sir' for so long that I really did not get off on it anymore – but because that was the sort of police force I had joined and that I cherished.

There were lots of faces I didn't recognise but some familiar ones – Julia Balfour and Andy Murray, two detective constables who had been stalwarts of the Levi Bellfield investigation, had volunteered to come and help, and also DCs Jim Wallace and Cathy Farrell who had been loaned to me from Counter-Terrorism, looking a little older but still as smart and as match-fit as they always had been as mainstays of my CID office in Chingford some fourteen years previously.

A few of the officers I did not know had separately

introduced themselves to me as they came in and made a point of congratulating me on the Levi Bellfield case; policing in the Met often being quite parochial it meant a lot to me that our successes on the other side of London had nevertheless resonated with colleagues elsewhere. I could not miss the opportunity of thanking them while still pointing out that it was now *our* time, time to do it again, time for them to be part of something special.

I started my briefing by suggesting an image I had used several times during the Bellfield investigation, imploring them to remember that what we were about to do would be the sort of success they would one day be telling their grand-children about. That it would be an honour, always, to be able to recount that you were a part of it. My operational input to the briefing was really confined to the high-level stuff – the overall intention, the mantra that we must show or leave no trace of our presence and, invoking Ellen and Thomas once more, a gentle but powerful reminder of why we were all there, what success would mean to all those lonely, vulnerable old people in south-east London.

The detail – who was going where, call-signs, equipment and vehicles – I left to a clutch of capable detective sergeants, introducing them by pointing out that they did this sort of thing every day and were therefore much more likely to get it right than some head-in-the-clouds pen-pusher DCI. This was met with a murmur of laughter, turning into a proper peal when I added that I would, though, always have that pen available to sign overtime and expenses claims. The briefing broke up at around ten o'clock, leaving the team of more than seventy experienced detectives upon which all my hopes now depended a generous hour to get settled in and vigilant at their observation posts for the start time of 11 pm.

I drove myself over to Vauxhall, leaving the car in the vast underground car park and heading up to Central 3000, our home for the duration – or at least until a terrorist or kidnap incident trumped Minstead and we were kicked out. Which throughout our surveillance operation was to be a constant, if entirely reasonable, threat. It was only the second time I had been inside the state-of-the-art control suite – the previous occasion being a week or so earlier when we had been planning the surveillance operation. It was an ultra-modern and impressive facility, the main room being an unbroken arc of desks with each console position having computer, radio and telephone facilities. These faced towards a wall dominated by a bank of large flat-screen displays, eighteen of them in two rows of nine, on to which could be projected feeds from CCTV, hidden cameras or computer screens. There were breakout rooms for meetings, a kitchen/dining area and an SIOs' room, which I suggested we used for our coats and bags. I was not going to be hiding away – I wanted to be in the room, living and breathing the tension and, I hoped, excitement.

We settled down and selected the CCTV pictures we wanted for the start, radio operators and intelligence staff readied their positions and we waited. Just before the 'go live' time of 11 pm each of the observation points (always referred to as O-P, their radio call-sign being O-P1, O-P2 and so on) reported that they were in position, checking at the same time that their signals were clear and communications were good. Unsurprisingly on what was a very cloudy night, our air support told us that they did not think they would be of much use until after 3 am, when the weather had been forecast to clear. Nearly twenty pairs of officers in bedrooms, empty houses and even two in a church tower, supported by mobile teams on the ground and in the air nearby, were watching over an area of just less than two square miles, north of the A232 in Shirley, with Orchard Way running north to south as its spine.

It seemed incredible to think that the Night Stalker had committed so many offences in this relatively small area. The roads of our 'plot' – to use the cop slang – were exclusively residential, solid 1930s family houses, as I've said, of the sort he chose to attack. The demographic of the area was such that there was very little movement, pedestrian or vehicular, after midnight and those residents who did venture out for a late dog walk were overwhelmingly white. There was every chance that, if the Night Stalker walked the final part of his journey to his victims – as we had every reason to believe he did – we would see him relatively easily. It was the decisions to be made then, when we had a possible suspect in front of us, that would make or break the plan.

Waiting for something to happen during a static surveillance operation is a strange experience. You know that hours of boredom will only be punctuated by moments of interest and that most of those will turn out to be nothing. Nevertheless, you must be vigilant and prepared to observe, record and evaluate those sporadic events as they arise. There is always tension and expectation in the air and you can almost see concentration on the officers' faces; for me added to that were personal feelings of real trepidation. This was a huge and expensive operation, being watched from the very top of the Met. There was absolutely no guarantee it would work. And if it did not it was all on me.

The night came and went, a handful of cars and even fewer

pedestrians had passed through the plot but nobody even slightly resembling the Night Stalker had appeared. Of course, I had not really expected it to work on the first night but naturally a small part of me had thought it might. Or at least, had certainly hoped that way.

I left Vauxhall at around 5.30 am and drove home to sleep for a few hours before returning to Lewisham for 10.30. It was an unfortunate quirk of the calendar that the start of the proactive operation coincided with Nathan Eason being away on a two-week SIO course. So after the first two nights that was it, I wouldn't have him there for a fortnight. It would have been grossly unfair to pull him from the course (although, typically, he had offered and theoretically I could have required it) as there was no knowing when he would get another opportunity. I was not about to treat somebody who had given me so much like that.

But we had agreed in the planning that either he or I should always be in the control room when the surveillance was running – we hoped there would be decisions arising that should only fall to him or me to take. After the first couple of nights when we both attended, I had little choice but to do it alone until he became available again. Since I could not just abandon the day-to-day duties I had with Minstead as the SIO, the various meetings and other Command business that I had to attend to, I had to be at Lewisham during the day as well. It was a case of gritting my teeth and getting on with a fifteen-hour split shift for each of the next fourteen days. My working day was roughly 10 am to 4 pm at Lewisham, then home and back for the night stint from 9 pm to 6 am. Repeated if not ad infinitum, then at least for two weeks.

The day team at Lewisham knew I had been up all night and so did not disturb me, but what I discovered when I arrived in the office the next morning made me think I really would not have blamed them if they had. (Indeed, that was one of my personal rules: never, ever, be displeased when somebody calls you out of hours, even if you think they did not really need to. Because it will only result in them being reluctant to call in future, when what they had to say might that time have been really important.)

The Night Stalker had been busy that night. While we were all watching the Shirley plot he had committed three burglaries. The first two – one an attempt where he didn't gain entry – were near Elmers End, less than half a mile from the north-west corner of the plot. The third was even closer to 'our' border, just a few hundred yards to the south-east, towards the rear of grounds of the Bethlem Royal Hospital. I picked up the map, staring at it, incredulous. First it was so close, so very near to having been right under our noses. But the next thought brought me goose bumps. The first two crimes were just yards apart, but the third was more than two miles away. And the time span between them – less than thirty minutes from the second to the third – made it virtually impossible that he could have got between them by foot. He had to have been driving and the most logical, practically only possible, route would have been down Orchard Way – straight through the middle of our plot. We had definitely seen no black male pedestrians, so one of the handful of cars we had watched go past just a few hours ago had to have been driven by the Night Stalker.

I had been here before, knowing that the suspect must have been driving on a road at a particular time. CCTV had been my saviour back then but that was on busy roads with lots of cameras mounted on the buses and in commercial premises. What about Orchard Way, which had neither? Kicking myself slightly for not having commissioned a CCTV survey of the area before we started, I asked the first two officers I could find to drop everything, head to Orchard Way and take a slow walk up and down to see what they might turn up. So as not to risk blowing the surveillance, we concocted a bland cover story that they were looking for a car which had escaped after a police pursuit. Looking at the map once more I pointed out that there were a couple of schools on Orchard Way which might prove fruitful but I stressed that the whole road needed to be explored. Before I left for home at 4 pm they had returned, slightly animated, with a VHS cassette and a couple of DVDs in their hands.

Chapter 17

CHASING CARS AGAIN

The VHS tape was from a private house, coincidentally the home of a man who had worked for the Metropolitan Police who was only too pleased to help us. The officers related how they had felt bad about giving him the white lie of the pursuit but I told them I was nevertheless pleased they had stayed strong, even with a former colleague, and preserved our cover. As in Farnaby Road months before, his camera was again trained on the cars on the drive, but its field of view took in part of the road at its top left. The recording showed a car parking up on Orchard Way and a figure leaving it, only to return and drive away about an hour later. The time of the footage matched the reported times of the third burglary exactly. But the frames were scratchy and blurred, typical of an old system using a worn tape, and in any case the important action was restricted to just a few pixels in the corner. As confirmation that our man had been on Orchard Way it was invaluable but as a means of identifying him it was useless.

The DVDs from the school were more promising. The camera set up to monitor the school drive showed passing vehicles – or at least the top half of them. The quality was better, though still not marvellous, and by working our way backwards from the time of the other footage we could see what had to be our target vehicle, a car containing the Night Stalker, passing south on Orchard Way at 5.13 am on its way to the scene of the third burglary. It was a silver or grey car; from its roofline we thought it was possibly an estate car or more probably a people carrier or MPV. I knew where our next enquiry would have to be made – Andy Wooller at the Transport Research Laboratory at Thatcham was my go-to person for identifying cars, having turned up trumps for me in the Levi Bellfield case and indeed during a couple of less well-known investigations as well. I made the call, he agreed to have a look at an emailed photo and within twenty minutes I had my answer. He was 75 per cent certain it was a Vauxhall Zafira, the B model with updated styling, which had been sold from 2005 and was still a current model.

Excited that we were making progress, yet at once daunted by what I knew would be a huge number of these popular models on the road, I had a strong feeling of déjà vu. I thought of the hundreds of hours we had put into proving that Bellfield had been driving the Courier van and the Vauxhall Corsa, and knew that to repeat that, while still responding to new offences and maintaining the widespread surveillance, was going to be impossible. It might be, I thought, that resources needed to be taken out of the surveillance, if it seemed that finding the Zafira was to be our best chance. I kept that thought firmly to myself and mused on it round the M25 as I popped home for dinner and a shower before I returned for the 9.30 pm briefing, before that working day's night leg.

It was somewhere near to Clacket Lane Services that it struck me. Come on, Colin – remember Minstead Lite. We had no need to prove the Night Stalker had been driving that Zafira, we could just use the knowledge that he had access to it to find out who he was. Remembering from Bellfield that the key might be to find those used – as opposed to registered – in the area local to the Minstead offences, I mentally drafted a plan. Educate the team on the differences between Zafira Bs and the old A model, get from Vauxhall the definitive dates of registration for the first of the improved models and have the team simply note the numbers of every one they saw during their normal travels, on or off duty. That would generate a list of cars which the intelligence team could work on to try to find keepers or drivers who fitted the Night Stalker's profile and thus throw up potential suspects. And that could be done alongside our current operations. I could give the surveillance a few weeks to see if it did work and then if not, or if other demands meant we had to abandon it, we could revert to the tough task of a more formal elimination of Zafira drivers. It somehow felt good, for once, to have a fallback, as much as I was willing that I would never actually have to use it.

The briefing that night was, therefore, not the repetitive affair it might otherwise have been. As well as 'more of the same' from the previous night, there was new material. Not just the offences and our new interest in Zafiras – but also the realisation that the Night Stalker might drive through the plot; indeed we could be certain that he already had. Although having been so close but failing was crushingly disappointing, there was enormous encouragement to be found in knowing that we were obviously, probably, operating in the correct area. The fact that he had been there on our very first night raised hope, and the optimism that this really might work was the main thrust of what I asked the team to believe. Somebody, betraying a laudable excess of optimism, remarked, 'It is only a matter of time.' I wanted to believe that and for them to as well, but knew more objectively my own, unspoken, belief was more that 'Time will tell.'

As I was googling images of 2005-onwards Vauxhall Zafiras so that I could prepare a briefing sheet for the team to carry around as a reference to make certain they were looking for the correct cars, there was a gentle knock on my open office door. It was Nathan, arriving early at the office prior to the briefing for what would be his last day before embarking on his training course. Like some others on the team, he looked unusually excited.

'I just heard. Brilliant, isn't it? Won't be long now before we have him in the bin.'

I stopped my cutting and pasting and looked at my DI, pausing as I considered how to give him the reality without curbing his obvious enthusiasm.

'It's a step forward, it might even turn into a leap. But don't be fooled, if this is the key to solving it there is a huge mound of work to be got through.'

Nathan looked puzzled so I continued.

'We now know the type of car he was using last night. If it is his, or one he uses regularly, it might take us to him. But my man at the TRL reckons there are getting on for fifty thousand of them on the road and, given the lack of detail or colour in the pictures, he might have a hard job eliminating very many on paper for us.'

'Yeah, but this is, this was how you got Bellfield, isn't it? I mean, you know how to do it?'

'Yes, it was how we got him and of course that means I do know how to do it. But that also means I know what a Herculean task it would be.'

He furrowed his brow and tilted his head slightly, inviting me to go on.

'Look, we had twenty-five thousand vans to look at and the one we wanted had some really distinctive features. And we never even really scratched the surface. It was only when other enquiries threw it up that we found out which of them it was. Then there were about twice as many Vauxhall Corsas but again we had enough detail to eliminate most of them on paper. We ended up with one hundred and seventy-eight to find and yes, we did it – but that whole process took more than a year.'

Almost completely deflated now, Nathan enquired, 'So what's your feeling on this, then?'

'If we have to eliminate fifty thousand cars with nothing else to go on then it is an almost impossible task, not least because of the staffing it would need. We can't even think about preparing for it while we are doing the surveillance.'

'It's very much Plan B then?'

'Nathan, I'm not even sure it is Plan B. I am sure it would be marginally better than DNA swabbing, but then really only just.'

He said nothing but the look on his face spoke for him. I could see he was not convinced, so I tried to explain.

'You have to trust me on this – I've been there. If it comes to it, maybe it is a way forward, but I am sure that we have to give the surveillance a chance to work first. If we really need to, we'll do the car thing but don't underestimate the difficulty. It will be a proper slog. So, we do need to curb the enthusiasm for it that might be growing in the team; we need their minds firmly fixed on the surveillance.'

Nathan smiled and muttered that of course I would know, that he understood and he would be with me on this one. I responded saying that was exactly as I knew it would be, he was always with me.

He changed tack. 'How are you going to cope doing the work of two men then?'

'That's usually followed up with "Laurel *and* Hardy", isn't it?' I responded, calling on an old Met joke.

Nathan chuckled and said, 'No, it will be a bit tough, at your age…'

'Yeah, thanks for that.'

'Seriously, Colin, as soon as the course is over and I can I'll be back to do my bit.'

'Yes, I know you will, can't be helped and I know you'd rather be here than there anyway. As soon as you can then I'll be very grateful, but in the meantime just make sure you pass.'

'You don't have to pass courses these days, it's 2009,' he replied with his usual dry cynicism as he got up and started on his way home.

Chapter 18

THE SECOND NIGHT OF SURVEILLANCE

The administration, the housekeeping, of the operation ran smoothly, in some ways surprisingly so. Everyone turned up on time, nobody complained about the hours, the conditions or the equipment. They arrived, got briefed and departed to their OPs with the minimum of fuss. This was possibly one of the advantages, for me as leader, of having a team made up entirely of experienced and committed detectives, there to make a difference and not just on a break from their usual job and for a load of overtime. I had not the slightest doubt that every single one of them really wanted to succeed.

I drove myself to Central 3000 from Lewisham, still needing to rely on the satnav in what was my least-familiar part of the capital. Yes, I had a thousand things on my mind as I did so, but despite that, despite having my rank and role, despite being in my twenty-ninth year of service, I was still, when it came down to it, just a policeman on duty, driving a police car. Perhaps it was my keeping an eye out for grey Zafiras, as I had just exhorted the team to do, that heightened my awareness, as I did spot something.

Alongside the Zafiras there was another model of car in which we maintained a minor interest. You will recall the silver Peugeot 406 saloon that had been captured on CCTV near the HSBC cash machine in Westmoreland Road where the Night Stalker had made his attempt to take money from a victim's account under the gaze of his own e-fit. The area was busier than Orchard Way and the link between the 406 and him was nowhere near as strong, but nevertheless we maintained some interest in these vehicles. Who knew, he might easily have had access to two cars.

As I made my way through Peckham towards Camberwell to go on to Vauxhall I saw a silver 406 parked at the kerb. As I drew closer to it a man went to the driver's door. He was black, aged about forty and, as I passed, turned full-face to watch me pass before opening the door. I got a good look at him in the streetlights and our eyes met. He looked very much like one of the few Minstead e-fits that showed a complete face.

After he drove off and followed me, I deliberately dawdled in the traffic so that he passed. I had no easy means of communication with the Minstead office at that point and so to stop and speak to him I needed to engage the assistance of the local police. Which gave me a problem I ought to have foreseen before I pressed the transmit button on the radio: I had not the faintest idea of the name of the road I was on.

'MP, MP from Metro Charlie one one six nine, active message.' It had been so long since I had needed to ask for assistance like this that I was almost surprised I could remember the procedure – and indeed my personal Met-wide call sign.

'Metro Charlie one one six nine go ahead,' the radio operator immediately replied before, I imagined, looking up on his e-directory to learn who the officer behind this unusual and little-used call sign might be. And checking just how senior his caller was.

'MP from Metro Charlie one one six nine, I'd like assistance from a marked vehicle please, to stop a grey Peugeot 406 saloon, registration P Papa Two Two Six R Romeo H Hotel W Whisky. One occupant… stand by…'

'Colin, you bloody idiot! Where are you?' I thought. The man in the Peugeot saved my blushes over the airwaves by turning right, not only enabling me to catch a glimpse of a street sign but also giving me an excuse for my hesitancy.

'H…he's just turned into Benhill Road, SE5, heading north.' A quick check of the arrow on the satnav had given me our direction of travel and made my commentary appear seamlessly confident.

The operator at Scotland Yard relayed my request and the only free unit that offered up to assist had a call-sign which began 'Trojan', signifying to me that it was an ARV – an armed response vehicle. Which of course I would not have requested and had no reason to suspect I would need, but nevertheless made me feel a little more comfortable. They suggested they were five minutes away and asked me to keep them updated as I followed. Of course the man in the Peugeot was completely unaware of this. It was no chase, just me gently trying to keep tabs on him until help arrived.

We went through a few back streets, my commentary faithfully relaying their names to my would-be colleagues. The area changed from Edwardian terraces to a mixture of light industrial units and estates of low-rise flats. Then the last thing I wanted to happen did: the 406 pulled up to the kerb in a car park between blocks of dreary-looking red-brick flats, which someone on the radio with access either to a map or local knowledge far better than mine soon assured me was the Elmington Estate.

Decision time. The ARV said they would be with me in two minutes, I was alone with no personal protective equipment and needed to stop him from disappearing into the flats for ever. The car, I had by this time been informed, had no current keeper registered against it. It was very dark. I had no idea where I was and I was much too tired to run and far too old to fight. But I would never have forgiven myself if it turned out to have been him and I had let him go. I had been here before, a good number of times. You do something to get the job done that you know, objectively, is not really safe but that you know – or at least hope – 99.9 per cent of the time will turn out absolutely fine.

I thought the best answer might be the 'He's just a middle-aged bloke in a Golf, certainly not a copper' approach.

'Hello, mate, very sorry to bother you but can you help me, please?' It was an entirely neutral opening so that if he responded at all aggressively, I could just default to asking for directions.

He beamed a smile and asked, 'Yes, boss, you lost?' in a thick, sweet Bajan accent. It was truly one of the least threatening things I had ever heard.

'Well, yes I am, I suppose. But that's not why I wanted to talk to you,' I confessed, emboldened that this apparently happy and approachable man was never going to turn on me.

'You see, I am a police officer and I just think you might be able to help me.'

'Of course, boss, if I can help then I always will, y'know.'

Just as I was about to explain we heard the sirens and a large, striped and flashing BMW X5 turned the corner, drawing an almost double-take stare from the pair of us.

'Hey, are they all for me?' Peugeot-man looked aghast as I quickly gave then the universal waving hand signal that all was well.

'Yes, sort of,' I truthfully told him. 'Well, no all for me, really. Don't worry, let me explain…'

Like virtually everyone in south-east London, David McLean had heard and read about the Night Stalker, and like virtually everybody else he wanted nothing more than for us to catch him, so he was entirely comfortable that I had wanted to speak to him. And it turned out that he had a rock-solid alibi for the previous night and so I did not even need to bother to ask him for a DNA sample – when I told him this, he gave a chuckle again and explained that we already had his DNA anyway, from when he got caught with 'a little bit o' weed'. We said our most pleasant goodbyes and I had just arrived and parked my car at Vauxhall when the mobile rang. It was the intelligence DS from Central 3000.

'Where are you guv'nor? It's getting a little bit exciting here.'

'Not exactly been dull where I am either,' I retorted. 'I'll see you very soon, twenty seconds tops.'

Within half of that I had swiped in and half-jogged into the control room. What I found was remarkable. One of the jobs for the intelligence desk was to monitor the messages and calls coming into police all across south-east London. The purpose was to see if there were any incidents which might conceivably be Minstead-related, so we could keep an eye on them. Such monitoring was possible because all the calls and then every action taken as a result are logged and recorded on a computer system. Introduced in the 1980s and then named 'Computer Aided Despatch', the acronym CAD was now the common term; 'CAD' meaning the whole system, with each message individually and slightly confusingly also being known as 'a CAD'.

The team had picked up a CAD originating in Lambeth, some six miles north as the crow flies from the Minstead plot and, it was to turn out, at a location which was the furthest north that a Minstead offence was ever recorded. The local control room officers entered each new event on to the computer log as a quite incredible story unfolded.

A woman in her early seventies who lived alone in a detached house was in bed when, at about 11.30 pm, she heard a sound she recognised. It was her unlocked side gate opening and closing. She then heard a sharp noise from her side door and – correctly – concluded that somebody was breaking in. Terrified but maintaining a remarkable clarity of thought and expression, she took her mobile phone from the bedside table and dialled 999. Talking in a stage whisper behind a cupped hand she had relayed the information to the police live as it happened, giving a running commentary which was typed out for us to read, as she heard the intruder gain access, go from room to room on the ground floor and then, chillingly, the log reflected her transition into panic as she reported hearing the weight of his tread on her stairs.

The local police, for their part, had reacted swiftly. Officers were assigned immediately and indeed arrived at her house within four minutes of her call being put through. They had, at the instruction of their controller, maintained a 'silent approach', that is keeping their sirens off and extinguishing blue lights before entering her road – so as to minimise the warning and maximise their chances of apprehending the burglar.

As they arrived, they were only just too late. The Night Stalker had found the victim in her bedroom and seen that she was still speaking on her mobile. He had been smart enough to realise that he was in trouble and had grabbed the phone roughly from her grasp, spitting a few swear words at her as he turned and fled back down the stairs, back the way he'd come and out into the street. Her house was close to a T-junction. Using the street cunning we were getting to know he had in abundance, he chose to run away from this, where the road was straight and he could see for some distance that there were no police approaching.

Indeed, they were coming but from the other direction, and the first of them, a response car with two male officers, arrived with a chirp of tyre squeal round the corner from the T-junction, less than thirty seconds behind the Night Stalker. The events then unfolded as follows…

The driver of the car spotted the fleeing figure on the pavement ahead.

'There he is!'

He accelerated after him. The passenger officer (known as the operator) unfastened his seat belt, carefully guiding the buckle back over his radio, stab-vest and bulky equipment so it was out of the way for his anticipated and inevitable hasty exit. The seat belt warning ping from the car chimed, slowly for a few seconds and then more quickly, stridently, almost matching the PC's rising heartbeat and amplifying the tension in the car. The fleeing figure swerved off the pavement, across the drive of a detached house before vanishing in the space between the building and a slatted fence.

The operator, a fit PC in his mid-twenties, exited the car while it was still moving, urging not the suspect but his driver to 'Stop, Stop, STOP!'

He bailed out and gave chase, tearing off down the side of the house after the Night Stalker, launching into an epic foot chase, while his driver reported on the radio that the 'suspects on premises' call had now changed to 'PC chasing suspects'. Funny how it always seems to be suspects (plural) on the radio no matter how many there are.

Chasing on foot, wearing a stab vest and carrying several kilos of other gear, is never easy even for the fittest officers. While adrenalin might help speed and even stamina, aside from running the pursuer needs to be able intermittently to advise of progress and location on the radio. The nearby colleagues need keen ears to translate the resulting garbled and breathless updates so as to manoeuvre themselves into a position to be able to assist.

The urgent, higher-pitched tones of the driver yelped out of the radio monitor at Central 3000 before I could even take a seat, as the radio link was put through.

'MP, MP from Lima X-ray Three One, active message. PC 1263 is chasing suspects on foot, in an alley from Douglas Road, north towards Holden Avenue...'

The excited commentary from the loudspeaker jolted me from whatever inconsequential conversation I was engaged in.

I knew from the dialogue what was happening, but why was it important to us? I turned to Michele, one of the detectives loaned to me to run the control and, unflappably, she explained in her soft Northern Irish tone.

'We were monitoring a CAD from LX, a foot-chase following a break-in at the home of an elderly woman. The suspect has decamped and we've just patched into the local channel which is now linked to the main set' – the 'main set' being one of the force-wide radio channels.

I moved closer to the monitor and the next thing I heard was the fast, crunching tread of footfalls, then: '... east in Holden Avenue... EAST HOLDEN AVENUE...'

The Met control room operator, call sign MP, parroted the report with the calmness and clarity customary to all those in that role: 'East in Holden Avenue received, keep the commentary going, MP over...'

Having no idea at all where the action was taking place I asked if we had a map. A few presses of a keyboard later and one of the wall screens changed from a deserted still life of a suburban street to a richly coloured street map upon which the streets already shouted by our breathless colleague were readily visible.

The controller spoke again: 'Any unit have a description of the suspects in this foot chase on Lima X-ray, MP over?'

A different voice responded, from the wailing sirens in the background not quite drowning the high-revving engine it was very obviously the driver, less urgent than in his original request for help:

'MP from Lima X-ray three one, one male, IC3, dark clothing... that's about all we have...'

Quickly taking stock, I realised we had a black man being chased, having broken in at the home of an elderly lady, late at night. It was very promising. A dozen officers in Central 3000 were transfixed, seldom daring to breathe let alone speak, desperate for the next gasped words we heard to be the almost-magical phrase 'suspect detained MP' – and for the hunt to be over.

We were not to know just what a saga the chase had become. Our PC, not knowing he was the bearer of all our immediate hopes, ignoring the hindrances offered by his stab vest and a few kilos of gear, was vaulting fences, landing in back gardens clogged with toys, garden furniture and barbecues, each one forming part of a treacherous obstacle course in the dark. Yet still he gave us hope.

'Into back gardens, Holden Avenue, north,' he breathlessly and gamely continued, his controller relaying the information and trying to organise assistance:

'North in back gardens, Holden Avenue received. All units from MP, looks like he'll emerge into Gondor Road, Gondor Road, MP over.'

With his heart feeling like it might burst through the stab vest at any second, the PC continued the chase. While he could still see his quarry, while he was yet able to hear that scampering up ahead, no amount of pain would stop him. Setting off a cacophony of barking, he cleared another garden fence and was, as predicted, into Gondor Road, his sweat-blurred eyes casting around frantically, then locking onto the flitting, wraith-like figure of the Night Stalker. He set off again, as quickly as his tired limbs would allow, straining to hear the approaching salvation of colleagues rushing to assist him. The sirens were near now, but still not close enough. He barked an update into the Airwave radio swinging against his chest on his stab vest.

'Gondor Road… Gondor Road west… stand by… he's into the park!'

He saw the Night Stalker vanish from the pavement ahead bolting through the gate of a park. There he was, a shadow, a silhouette, barely discernible as he darted through the swings and slides and weaved to avoid the picnic benches of a boarded-up cafe.

The Night Stalker's luck was in again; at least it looked like it, for if it were a deliberate ploy then his local knowledge must have been quite comprehensive. The park he had entered provided a shortcut to a railway footbridge. A combination of a small brook and the railway line meant that most of the nearby residential streets were cul-de-sacs; any assisting officers in vehicles would have to make a huge, time-consuming detour to get to the other side of the bridge.

In Central 3000 we were still listening intently as the realisation dawned upon us that the outcome was by no means certain. The Night Stalker ignored the railway bridge, choosing instead to ford the stream. The game and determined officer followed his prey through the shallow water course, clambering up its muddy bank and continuing with his desperate and obviously exhausted roll call of street names.

'… Bailey Gardens… Cricketfield Road… Phoenix Street… Pandora Road… he's over a fence into some sort of yard…'

The chase continued, through piles of rubble and sand, both men dodging a hulking cement mixer. Drenched in sweat, feeling every shattering step of the two miles he had run, the officer was at the very end of his strength. He was running on pure adrenalin now. Ahead of him the clear but featureless outline of the Night Stalker scrambled up a digger, leapt from its roof and cleared the wall at the back of the builders' yard.

Mimicking the suspect, the officer vaulted high over the wall, landing hard on an unforgiving surface that jarred his aching legs. Looking swiftly around he saw that he had landed in a vast car park attached to a superstore. Wet tarmac gleaming eerily, bathed with green-and-orange light from its signs, fully illuminated even at this hour. Despite there being more ambient light than at any time since the officer had left the car, the Night Stalker was nowhere to be seen.

The constable picked himself up, heart thumping, casting his gaze hopefully around the empty expanse of smooth asphalt. Where did he go? There was nowhere to hide except four cars and a van dotted around the car park. Resisting the temptation to pick a direction, to trust to luck and set off again, he moved deliberately and silently over to the abandoned vehicles.

Kneeling down on the wet tarmac he started to peer under the five vehicles. No torch, the last thing he wanted to do was to set the chase off again. If the Night Stalker were hiding, well, let him hide until the troops arrived. Each car drew a blank, but then the van, with its higher ground clearance, was probably always the best bet. Did he spy movement or was it the sweat stinging his eyes? He shuffled over, silencing his radio and pulling out and racking his ASP baton as he neared the rear of the van; the reassuring click as its sections locked into place was familiarly comforting as it always was. Arcing around in one bold ready-for-anything movement – it was clear. This marathon pursuit – the hunter fuelled by determination, his quarry by self-preservation – was over and self-preservation had won by a whisker.

The atmosphere in Central 3000 was heavy. We simply did not know all that had happened, had received no new information since the officer went into the builder's yard. And, as much as we wanted to ask, wanted to press for an update, we knew we had to let the poor bloke take his time. When it came, the transmission was quiet, whispered almost, and paid no heed to correct radio procedure.

'I fucking lost him.'

No call signs, nothing but the desolate admission of a courageous young man who had given it everything he had but knew he had still come up just short. The bad language did not stop with him though; it was repeated in all corners of Central 3000. Incredible, was it not, how lucky this man proved to be? Every bloody time it seemed. There was of course still a chance – we knew he was out there in the general area somewhere, he must be. The radio transmissions once more became a model of propriety.

'MP, MP from 1263. Suspect lost, Creekside Retail Park, superstore car park,' in a firm but thin voice, laden with disappointment and frustration.

The controller instantly replied with the text-book response to a failed foot chase.

'1263 all received. Units to assist, please, a search for suspect, Creekside Retail Park. Is there any dog unit available, MP over?'

'Lima Zero, MP, ETA two minutes...' was the eager reply, the sirens in the background showing that the handler already meant business, probably anticipating the call.

As the CAD operator faithfully recorded on the message, the chase went on for more than two miles. From the street, through a park, over walls, through gardens, back on to the street, through an alley, over another fence, through a small river, then the builders' yard and eventually over a wall and into the car park. Despite the athletic prowess of the young chasing officer, he had been unable significantly to reduce the distance between himself and the Night Stalker and as he landed and scanned the empty expanse of tarmac, he saw the suspect had gone. An assault course of a pursuit; those of us old enough were recalling *The Krypton Factor*. Just who – what, indeed – was this man we were after?

As I read through the chronology of abbreviations and control-room speak to distil these facts, in my mind I was racing ahead. What did this mean? My first concern was that he might have changed his target area so significantly because the surveillance had leaked. I was so sure that we were watertight but, when you are using private residences, there is always the risk of a careless remark blowing your cover.

Beyond that, it seemed our target was incredibly fit. Did that have implications for our suspect profile – should we be concentrating on the lower end of the age range, as surely the impressive physical performance of the suspect pointed to a younger man? But perhaps more worrying was trying to imagine how the Night Stalker would react to this very, very close shave. Over the seventeen-year course of the case there had been a few long periods during which no offences had apparently taken place. What had prompted his inactivity then? Could it have been near misses like this, perhaps near misses not so obvious as this one, of which we were unaware? That, for me was, paradoxically the nightmare. As much as I ought to have wanted him to stop offending, I knew that if he did, the surveillance operation would be useless and we would be back to swabbing for DNA or, now, eliminating tens of thousands of Vauxhall Zafiras.

Only time, I concluded once again, would tell.

Chapter 19

'IT LOOKS LIKE WE GOT HIM'

After the Lambeth near miss was discussed at the third night's briefing, opinion was divided. Glass half-empty: it might spook him into inactivity. Glass half-full: it might drive him back to operating in the areas where he was more comfortable. The latter would, of course, play neatly into our hands. I wasn't sure which way he would sway and suggested we needed just to wait and see. The outcome was, in the event, that both views were to be correct in some way – but it was to take a couple of weeks for that to become apparent.

We carried on, night after night of this slick and intensive surveillance, the finest officers and equipment the Metropolitan Police could bring to bear, all concentrating hard on nothing. The Night Stalker had, evidently, simply stopped offending. I was concerned – not that the operation would fail if it continued, since I was absolutely confident that the Night Stalker would, one day, come back to the plot to offend. But who knew how distant in the future that might be? After all, he had in the past gone quiet for years. How long would I be allowed to keep the operation going? And even if the bosses remained sympathetic and committed, my worry was that fatigue would then set in and the team would become disheartened or complacent that nothing was going to happen. A combination of attitudes certainly not conducive to accurate and alert observation.

As I spent night after night listening to minimal radio communication and watching unchanging images of deserted residential streets it became obvious that our plot really was the sleepiest of suburbia. After midnight virtually nothing moved, the urban foxes and inquisitive cats providing the only frequent action. So under-used were the observing officers I was genuinely worried that they would take to sleeping, or that they would become so accustomed to nothing happening that they would fail to recognise it when it did.

About ten days into the operation, I was stood in Central 3000 watching empty screens when I was joined by an officer in full uniform; I did not know him but a glance at his epaulettes showed me his seniority. He introduced himself, without a hint of irony, as a chief superintendent from the covert policing branch. I went to say that I would have expected a much better disguise, but held back, sensing that the moment might not quite be right for my schoolboy humour.

'How much longer do you think we can keep this up?' he enquired of me, motioning towards the bank of screens with his mug of coffee.

I thought about it and bought a little time by slowly prefacing my reply with, 'Well, I suppose…'

Clearly, he was considering that the expense and disruption needed review given the lack of activity – and, indeed, of offences. I knew what I wanted to say but needed to pitch it correctly – neither bullish nor defeatist. I decided the burgeoning culture of back-covering within the police service might, for once, work to my advantage.

'… I suppose until somebody has the balls to call it off two days before he rapes or kills an elderly lady.'

My reply was both challenging and realistic. I wanted to make sure the risks of not continuing were clearly set out. He took a sip from his coffee and looked me in the eye.

'Hmm. Indeed!' he replied with a half-smile, as he wandered off to speak to the rest of the room.

Friday, 13 November 2009 ironically brought me some unexpected but much-appreciated luck. In the afternoon as I was eagerly anticipating my power nap, I got a phone call from Nathan Eason. He told me he had now finished his DI course and that meant he was again free to perform other duties. Despite being rostered to be on leave over the coming weekend, he suggested he should take on running the surveillance operation on Saturday and Sunday night, his customarily understated reasoning being 'You've had a bit of a time of it.' This was of course a very welcome offer; I was reaching exhaustion levels. I accepted without a second thought and as soon as I told Louise the good news she made immediate arrangements for my parents and children to visit us for lunch on Sunday 15th for a slightly belated celebration of my birthday, which had fallen on the previous Wednesday. I briefed Nathan of all the latest (non) developments over the phone, stressing the need to follow any suspects well away from the plot for a stop, but remarked also that, depressingly, the chances of that were looking increasingly unlikely. That was it, I was free for a change and could look forward to a proper weekend off.

Such was my feeling of freedom that I even watched England lose to Brazil in a football friendly on the evening of Saturday 14th, enjoying a glass or two of my favourite Irish whiskey as I did so and retiring to bed around 11 pm. I was looking forward to catching up on some sleep with, for a change, England's dire prospects for the following year's World Cup on my mind rather than the Night Stalker. I knew the operation was in Nathan's safest of hands. Despite this I could not break the habit of leaving my mobile charging on the bedside table (I still can't), silenced for everything but incoming calls.

It was perhaps somewhat inevitable in the scheme of things that my slumbers were interrupted at around half past one. Jolted into wakefulness, Louise and I simultaneously exclaimed 'Bloody hell!' as I answered.

'Colin, it's Nathan. It looks like we've got him.' My DI did not need to say anything else. Bolt upright, I tried to speak but found it hard to know what to say.

'Fuck, you're joking?'

'Do you think I'd joke about that?' He paused, 'Ever, really, but especially at one in the morning?'

Absolutely fair point, I thought. I asked how, who, where, what, when – dozens of questions spilling out in excitement and wonder and to which I knew Nathan would be unable, at this early stage, to provide answers with any certainty. But he was still able to give me the headlines.

A pair of the surveillance officers, a thoughtful and very well-regarded detective sergeant named Nathan Coutts and his colleague DC Jenkins, had noticed a Vauxhall Zafira as they walked to their observation point in Orchard Way. It was parked near the junction with a side street and the officers realised it had not been there on any previous evening since the operation had begun. They also saw that it was the 'correct' silver-grey colour and a face-lifted model. It had exactly the same appearance as the partial shot seen on the CCTV and complied with all the features I had pointed out in my briefing to try to turn the team into expert Zafira-recognisers.

Once ensconced behind the bedroom window of their empty house they had pointed it out to their colleagues, circulating its details to the nearby O-Ps, just making sure that all the team would be alive to its existence if it were suddenly to become any more interesting. After an hour or so they saw a black man jogging towards the car from Wilks Gardens. He got in and drove away, completely normally, to head north in Orchard Way.

In Central 3000, Nathan heard this and made all the right calls. The aerial support was asked to turn its attention to the Zafira just in case, the O-Ps along its route reported the car's progress as it passed them, and the mobile surveillance team at the edge of the plot sprung into action. This part of the plan was crucial; if a suspect needed to be stopped it was essential to do it as far away from the observation plot as possible. That way, if the suspect was found to be irrelevant it would be difficult for him to realise where he had first been seen and so there was much less chance of our operation – and most importantly its location – leaking to the public.

The surveillance team had followed him for around three miles, ending up in Witham Road, near to Beckenham Crematorium – ironically a residential street of terraced

1930s homes, typical Night Stalker territory. As this was the gateway to a maze of deserted suburban streets, the sergeant in charge of the surveillance team had sensibly decided it would be difficult to follow much further without 'showing out'. He took the decision to call the strike there and then. Whether the Night Stalker was intending to strike there again is of course unknown. Certainly, it was very much the sort of location he would have chosen, and we were to realise once he was identified that his direction was away from rather than towards his home. It is entirely possible that, having failed in his attempt in Shirley, he was seeking another possible victim. But he never got the chance. Pulled over to the side of the road, he got out of the car and tried to use his undoubted charm to talk his way out of it. Not that at that moment he could be sure what 'it' was; he had no way of knowing he had been tailed all the way from Shirley.

He had at first given the name Kelvin Grant, perhaps mindful to use his correct surname as the Zafira was ultimately for the use of his disabled wife Jennifer. He had presumably forgotten that, in the centre console, were a couple of his own credit cards, betraying his correct forename. When the searching officer found them he relented, explaining that Delroy was indeed his name but 'Everybody calls me Kelvin, y'know.' The cards, while useful, were not the greatest prize on offer. The surveillance officers had all been briefed and that briefing included the footage from the covert cameras at the Honor Oak Park cash machine. Therefore they were able to recognise the black balaclava in the glove compartment, the blue cagoule tossed on the passenger seat and the grey top with the black stripe over the sleeves in the boot all as belonging to the Night

Stalker. That the clothes were accompanied by a crowbar, a torch and what was later to prove the elusive screwdriver that had left so many distinctive marks at Minstead offences was the icing on the cake. Delroy Easton Grant was arrested and taken to Lewisham. Nathan Eason had indeed not been joking – it really did look like we'd got him.

I remembered the advice I had been given all those years ago when I did my own DI's course and invoked it, partly due to knowing it was likely to be fresh in Nathan's mind. The theory is that when an incident is obviously going to unfold over many hours its command should be continuous. Those in command should make sure that their presence is spread out across the whole period; usually this will be achieved by not having them on duty at the same time. Therefore, as Nathan was already there and working, I had no need to join him, but the principle said I should plan to go in later to relieve him, providing both continuity of command and important rest for the both of us. So that's what I suggested.

'OK, well, that's great news, great work, all of you. Shall I leave it with you and see you at about eight o'clock then?'

Nathan uttered a slightly surprised, 'Ooh,' but quickly recovered to say, 'Yes. Of course, yes. I'll see you then then.'

I am sure it was not what he had expected me to say, and almost instantly I regretted playing by the book this time. I wanted to be there, even if I was not strictly needed.

I ended the call and replaced the phone. Lying on my back I puffed my cheeks and exhaled noisily, staring unseeing at the ceiling in the almost-darkness. Excitement that we had succeeded, a large tinge of sadness that I was not there to see it, considerable apprehensiveness that the DNA might not get checked for a day or two. And some fear that the DNA might prove it was the wrong man. Don't be daft, Colin – what about the clothing? It is him. Would my birthday lunch be ruined after all? Like I cared, this was a better present than anything I could have imagined. The enormity of it started to come to mind. We had done it, after seventeen years of Minstead the new strategy had got him in seventeen days. Even at that early point I realised how much the media would like the symmetry of that line. I liked it, too. Loved it. The emotion, the feeling of pride and relief was similar to that I had felt when Levi Bellfield had been convicted. Not as intense – the truth was I had invested nowhere near as much time and energy in this one – yet the glow of success was still unmistakably familiar and hugely welcome. It really was what I went to work for.

All this was playing ping-pong in my brain, obviously silently, but Louise knew me well enough to know exactly what would be going on inside my head. I thought she was still awake, and probably that she had heard much of what I had been told in the silence of the bedroom. Obviously I knew she had heard what I had said.

She turned towards me and simply said, 'Who are you kidding?'

It was not the opening gambit I had expected but it was delivered in a completely friendly and happy manner, so I countered, 'Did you get any of that? They've got him.'

'Yes, of course I did. You've done it again. It is brilliant, you deserve it for all you've put into it. But there is absolutely no way on earth that you go back to sleep now, is there? Ignore what the book might say, get on in there and enjoy the moment.'

She was, obviously, absolutely correct. I could not conceive of ever wanting to sleep less than I did there at that moment. Within half an hour I was showered, dressed and pressing on down the M25, determined not to waste another second in getting to Lewisham to meet the Night Stalker.

When I arrived, I went straight to the custody suite and Adam Spiers introduced me to Grant. He was shorter and considerably older than I had imagined, probably five-eight at the most and clearly around fifty. His slim but muscular frame was clothed in the baggy white sweatshirt and jogging bottoms supplied to prisoners who had had their clothing seized, the Met-supplied ensemble completed by white Dunlop plimsolls.

Adam told Grant, 'This is the boss, Mr Sutton.'

Grant extended his right hand, respectfully bowed his head, and in his deep but surprisingly soft voice he said, 'Hello, sir.'

I could not miss the fact as he spoke that he had no top teeth in the front of his mouth, nobody could. The lengths he had gone to in covering his face from victims were instantly explained – while his general appearance was unremarkable, the second he opened his mouth he was unmistakable. I reflected also on the difference in attitude he displayed when compared to Bellfield: the serial killer's belligerence and abuse was replaced by the serial rapist's gentle respect.

I looked him up and down, saying quite deliberately, 'I am *so* pleased to *meet* you,' the stressed words clearly conveying the special meaning I was giving to that most ordinary of greetings. His manner was such – respectful and compliant – that I thought it was going to be possible to have some degree of rapport with him. Employing what some might protest as stereotyping but what in truth is just a regular tool for anyone who deals with other people in their professional life, I made a quick assessment. West Indian, in his fifties, and so of a generation before baseball and basketball had diverted the attention of the young in that part of the world away from cricket.

And there he was, clad in white from head to toe, so I asked him, light-heartedly, 'What are you doing then, batting or bowling?' motioning with my glance at his attire.

Instantly he twigged my meaning and he came alive, eyes widening and enthusiastically asking, 'Are you into cricket then, sir? I bet you don't still play.'

'Actually I do, occasionally, yes – still. Do you?' I hid my slight irritation that this man, clearly some years my senior, although just as obviously in better condition, had rather implied I was over the hill. But I will concede, at that moment and after the fortnight I had just had, I almost certainly looked well past it.

Grant was on ground he clearly relished and went on, 'Yes, yes of course I do. Bat *and* bowl.'

'Oh, good for you, my knees are shot, they don't let me bowl anymore, but I can still swing a bat. Well, as much as I ever could…'

He became almost animated. For a moment we were not the SIO and the serial burglar and rapist in a custody suite, we were chatting just like two blokes in the pavilion, sharing a jug of beer after a Sunday game.

He was not through with the cricket talk just yet, either.

'Tell me, sir, what do you think of England's chances in South Africa this winter?'

'I'd be happier if we had one more quick bowler, I suppose, but I think… Yeah, but we still have a great chance.'

'Yeah, man. That's exactly what I've been saying to the boys!'

This pleasant if rather bizarre interlude was interrupted by the custody sergeant, with customary patience and courtesy asking Mr Grant if he could have a signature on the label for his DNA sample, please – and we all crashed back to reality.

Having had a friendly, inconsequential chat about cricket in a custody office with a man who knew that the mouth swab he had just given was going to put him in prison for twenty or thirty years was just about the most surreal experience of my life. As I watched Grant carefully append his signature to an evidence bag I chuckled to myself, thinking how my father – who himself was a Met officer - had once said to me that every time you thought you had seen it all as a copper something else would turn up and confound you. And I remembered it as another reason why I loved The Job.

Our immediate concern was that Grant might have just committed an offence and there could be an injured victim lying somewhere in her house needing medical attention. Some of the team had already identified the burglary he was fleeing from when they had first seen him: a nearby bungalow with a pane of glass removed. The occupier there was suffering badly from dementia and had responded to their enquiry by saying that despite the obvious entry she had not been burgled and that they should, therefore, 'Fuck off!' Which they did, but this offence was ultimately charged as an attempted burglary and Grant convicted for it.

But what if there had been others previously that night? The Police and Criminal Evidence Act provides for such circumstances; it authorises an interview without the usual niceties and safeguards of a lawyer and disclosure where there may be a life at risk. Sensibly I think, we invoked this seldom-used provision and Grant was immediately asked the question. He gave the slightly chilling and ultimately untrue response:

'I haven't visited anywhere tonight.'

Chapter 20

'A GREAT DAY FOR THE METROPOLITAN POLICE'

There was of course a certain, understandable, euphoria that we finally had our man in custody; an obvious buzz and renewed enthusiasm as the team went about their work. Tiredness and the frustrations of the previous months and years were forgotten as we went through the tasks we all knew so well – but had lusted after, in this particular case, for so long. I had to take my usual half a step back from the process to make sure everything was being done correctly and in good time. The obvious urgency was to get Grant's DNA profile compared with Minstead crime scenes; despite our all being pretty convinced we had the right man, it was only once we had scientific confirmation that we could be sure. Arrangements were made with the DNA database in Birmingham to conduct an instant comparison as soon as we could get the sample there and so, not for the first time, I made a call to Scotland Yard to enlist the help of a traffic car to whisk the sealed bag containing Grant's mouth swab up the M1. As always, they were happy to oblige and I knew it would be delivered and completed just as fast as was humanly possible.

The officers in the custody suite at Lewisham had another sample to take – Grant's fingerprints. Although there were no outstanding marks from crime scenes for them to be compared with, we knew that Delroy Easton Grant had a criminal record and fingerprints on file, so they were required just to confirm that the man we had before us was really who he said he was. This was achieved some hours before we got the DNA result but was not itself without incident.

As Adam Spiers and DC Steve Purvis took him across in order to take a 'wet set' (an old-fashioned fingerprinting using ink and paper), he engaged them in a chatty conversation, during which he said, 'Don't know why you are bothering with this – you know I always wore gloves.'

This remark had obvious import – it was tantamount to an admission of guilt. Quite correctly the officers immediately made a note of it and invited Grant to sign it as correct. Predictably he declined, being sufficiently acquainted with the investigation process to know that would make the remark impossible to deny in future. There was nothing especially cynical about this, it is a relatively common phenomenon. Seasoned criminals know exactly what both they and the police can and cannot get away with and will comply and interact just within these boundaries. Equally, seasoned officers appreciate this for what it is and there is no real animosity because of it on either side.

But it was to turn out that this remark was not the best one: the most outrageous comment was uttered on the following day when DC Joe Crockford was delivering food to Grant in his cell. Incredibly, it seemed that he was trying to blame his son for his crimes. Joe said that as they were asking Grant if he was well and joking about the unpalatable nature of custody-suite meals, he had come out with a spectacularly unexpected attempt at deflection.

'You really want to have a look at my son, you know. His DNA is going to be the same as mine. It is hard for me to say, you know, but I really want to make sure you get the right man.'

Ignoring Grant's ignorance of the science, that it could only be a twin not a son who had an identical profile to his, this was a breath-taking attempt to land responsibility for his awful crimes not just on some other innocent man but on his own flesh and blood. Once I had got over the sheer impudence, the despicable cynicism of Grant's desperate advice, I thought about how we should respond. Although I knew there was no chance of the son's DNA matching, for the sake of a relatively simple swab and a submission it would be possible for us to prove so, conclusively. I instructed the team to make arrangements to find Grant's son and take a voluntary sample; it was rare enough for us to get an idea of possible lines of defence so early in the process and so a virtual no-brainer to make sure we could refute it just in case. Unsurprisingly, it was found that Grant Junior's DNA profile was not a match for the crime-scene profiles.

On the morning of the arrest, the sheer number of officers outside the custody suite made the Minstead team office a veritable hive of activity. We had put plans in place some weeks previously for an interview strategy and indeed a schedule of offences with which it would be possible to charge our suspect once we had him, even if the arrest yielded no evidence in addition to his DNA profile. Crucially for us there was an early offence where Grant had not only left his DNA but had also used a screwdriver to force a window, leaving marks in the frame as distinctive, under the scientist's microscope, as a fingerprint. By a logical chain, any offences where marks left at the entry point suggested the use of his favourite screwdriver could be taken to to be his work as conclusively as if he had left DNA there. These were reviewed and seven added to the original list, meaning he was to be interviewed with a view to charging a total of twenty-nine offences, including rape, indecent assault, burglary and theft, stretching from 1992 to 2009. There was a degree of discussion about just how many offences should be pursued.

Within the Met there was a feeling that we should make the eventual indictment as short as possible, making the pre-trial work easier while still ensuring he would be convicted of suitably serious, specimen offences. This approach troubled me, and I found an ally in Andrew Hadik, the excellent Senior CPS lawyer who had managed the Bellfield case for me. We had worked well together; I respected his attention to detail and knew I would have an extra layer of comfort and security if he were involved. I had therefore specifically asked that he be assigned to the case. He agreed that it was important to show as well as we could the scale of Grant's offending, bearing especially in mind that we were certain the offences we could prove represented only a fraction of the total number he had committed. I was sure this was the right thing to do at the time; the hindsight afforded us now by the John Worboys (the 'Black Cab Rapist') case (where only a few specimen charges were brought and there arose a real prospect of his being paroled until he was further charged with outstanding crimes) reaffirms that we came to the correct decision.

Sam and Debbie, the stalwart Minstead FLOs, were also incredibly busy. I had sat down with them and explained how, in the Bellfield case, we had tried as far as possible to include all known victims in the FLO network – even if we had not uncovered enough evidence to prosecute 'their' offences. And how, when presenting this strategy to the national FLO Conference, I had remarked that although it had worked and was indeed probably very good practice, it was something that would only ever be of use once in a generation. It never crossed my mind that anybody in the Met might need to do it again within a couple of years, never mind that it could once again be part of an investigation I was leading. Sam and Debbie were frantically calling victims, trying to make sure everybody who needed to know were told by us before the news was in the media. It should never be forgotten that, while some of his victims had passed on by the time he was arrested, many were still alive, still scarred by their experience and still fearful of his return. More than one elderly lady expressed her relief that, for the first time in years, she could go to sleep feeling safer that night.

One of my personal priorities was to tell Simon Morgan of the arrest. I knew that he must have been told by somebody else on the team already – I would have been truly shocked if that had not been the case. Nevertheless, I knew that I had to do so, formally and without significant delay. Once it got to a reasonable hour (if 7.30 on a Sunday morning when you are not working can ever be considered reasonable), I called him at home. He was of course elated and, wanting to avoid any awkwardness, I mentioned a couple of times that I would tell him more when he arrived at Lewisham – proceeding on the basis that we both knew he was going to be coming in and that it was precisely what I expected him to do. I had also expected one of his first questions, if not the very first, to be, 'Was he in the system?' In layman's terms, was he known to the enquiry, was he a nominal entry in the HOLMES database and, most crucially, was he on the list of suspects who were due to be DNA screened? Because that would give an answer to the question, would Minstead have ever got him if the strategy had not changed? For that reason, before I called him I had the search done. What I found was disturbing and so was one of the things I suggested we spoke about in person. But I had to tell him the bottom line – which was that, 'Yes, there was a Delroy Grant with an address the same as our suspect but a different date of birth, listed as nominal N253 in the HOLMES account.' And that he was marked as having been eliminated because his DNA profile did not match that left by the Night Stalker at the crime scenes. Exactly how that situation had come about was unclear but it was certainly something we would need to get to the bottom of over the coming days and weeks.

Simon Morgan came in to Lewisham and I told him that, as far as I was concerned, it was something for which he had been longing for many years and that it was 'his day'. I left him to speak to those above us in the organisation and to deal with the media liaison. By about 4 pm I realised there was little else I could add that afternoon; Nathan Eason had returned from his post-night duty rest and so I concluded I ought to go home. I knew there was a house full of family there delaying

Sunday lunch and my birthday presents and, quite honestly, I was drained but wanted to share what emotions I had left with them.

As I drove around the M25, the phone in the cradle lit up with an unfamiliar number. Notwithstanding that I stabbed the answer button and heard a cheery, clear and unmistakably Lancastrian voice.

'Hello Colin, it's Paul Stephenson, I'm calling from the Punjab.'

An unorthodox greeting that caused my heart to jump. As old and experienced as I was, it was still a shock to get a personal call from the Commissioner, let alone one when he is at a conference halfway round the globe.

'I just wanted to congratulate you on your success and to thank you for what you have achieved. You know, Dick Fedorcio [the Met Head of Media] is with me and he has summed it up perfectly with a line I am giving to the press – "It is a great day for the Metropolitan Police."'

I mumbled some appreciative and respectful responses, told him how wonderful the team on the surveillance had been and how those above me but below him had been so supportive to make it happen. At least I think I did. To be honest although I remember his words with the clarity that their momentous importance merits, I cannot really be sure what I said to him. The whole press line I was later to read was:

This is one of the greatest days for the Metropolitan Police. Millions of man hours have gone into this. To get a breakthrough like this takes your breath away. The best bit is it did not come from a tip-off or DNA screening but from old-fashioned detective work. It makes you proud to be a cop.

This cop was certainly feeling very proud, the feeling of success and appreciation I felt will stay with me for ever. It was the moment I realised I really had done it again. When I got home there was the expected backslapping and cheering from Louise, Kat, Joe and my parents, and the birthday champagne had an even better than usual taste.

But perhaps the other thing I remember most fondly happened just after we sat down to eat, as the news of the arrest had broken beyond Lewisham. A one-word text from an officer from the Bellfield team who had left a few months previously on promotion to Detective Sergeant. It just read 'LEGEND!' Maybe the description was exaggerating my reputation a bit, but the sentiment was unmistakable. The appreciation from other detectives meant the whole world to me.

Chapter 21

TEN WASTED YEARS

The question of whether or not Delroy Grant was 'in the system' was an obvious one to ask but proved a complex one to answer. Strictly, I suppose, the answer would be 'sort of, yes'. But that fails to convey the horror show that had gone on a decade earlier – and that led to dozens more offences with the inevitable dozens of further victims. The sad truth is that Delroy Grant *should* have been in the system – and ought to have been arrested, convicted and imprisoned – in 1999, at the very start of the spree he had gone on during that year's summer.

In late May 1999, a burglary took place overnight at a house in Bromley. The burglar removed an air vent from a window, entered the house and stole property. The elderly lady who lived there was in bed, asleep, during the crime and had no knowledge of it until she awoke just before half past six the following morning. She immediately called the police and an officer attended later that morning, accompanied by a scenes-of-crimes officer. The scientific examination yielded no evidence and the initial investigating officer undertook house-to-house enquiries. He found nothing had been seen and that there was no CCTV in the street. His report entered on to the Crime Recording and Information System (CRIS) at Bromley Borough listed the missing property and noted that the victim, despite not having seen the intruder, was traumatised. The CRIS process was followed through with the crime entry being classified as 'burglary dwelling' and screened in for investigation by the local burglary squad.

A few days later, on 31 May 1999, the victim's son contacted the burglary squad with some new information. A neighbour who had been out during the initial house-to-house enquiries had told him that he had seen a suspicious man in the street late in the evening when the burglary occurred. Moreover, the witness had seen the man's car, describing it as a grey BMW saloon. Crucially, he had noted the registration number. A check on the number revealed that it was a grey BMW 535 and the registered keeper was Delroy Grant of Brockley Mews, London SE4. This of course is the name and address of the man we arrested ten years later.

When spoken to by the burglary squad officer to whom the crime had been allocated, the neighbour was able to give more detail. Although he could not describe the man's build or even race, he had seen him sitting in the car, pulling a balaclava or similar over his head and putting on a pair of gloves. He then watched as the suspect left the car, gently closing the door, and walked over towards the victim's house.

Armed with this knowledge, the investigating officer went back to the police station and started to interrogate databases to find what information was stored under the name Delroy

Grant. She found that there were two men with that name, obviously with separate criminal record files, on the Police National Computer. Each record showed a different address, date of birth and of course a different unique Criminal Records Office (CRO – now called PNCID) number. These personal records also showed whether a criminal's DNA profile was on the database. One of them, Delroy Easton Grant, had a last known address listed as being in Leicestershire but the other, plain Delroy Grant, was shown as living in London. The Leicester man had no DNA profile shown but the London Delroy Grant had a confirmed profile.

Perhaps understandably, she assumed that the man upon whom she should focus her interest was the latter – the one in London, oblivious to the fact that Delroy Grant from Brockley Mews, the registered keeper of the suspect BMW, had indeed lived in Leicester when he had last been arrested in the early 1990s. It was a natural assumption to make – I think any investigator would have *started* with the man that was most local – but it was also one which ought at some point to have been checked, tested and confirmed so that one of the possibles could be eliminated with certainty. She would also have been able to note that there was an age difference of more than fifteen years between the two men – another fact which would have helped distinguish them. However, since the witness could not describe the suspect's age it was not a feature which could assist her at that stage.

By chance, this officer had, in a previous role, assisted in caring for the victim of a Minstead assault. She was therefore personally very aware of the crime series and the features of the Minstead offences. Given the time of the burglary, the method of entry and the age of the victim, she took the sensible decision to make the Minstead team aware of what she had found. Thus, she sent details of the offence and the suspect to a detective constable at Minstead who made an assessment that there were insufficient 'markers' to be sure it was a Minstead offence and so the investigation should remain with the Borough Burglary Squad.

Each officer then made further database entries which showed clearly what had happened. The Bromley officer made an intelligence report, a paragraph of which read:

The vehicle is registered to a Delroy Grant, of Brockley Mews. On PNC there is a [similarly named man], CRO number XXXXXX. I have liaised with XX CID who state that he is unknown on XXXXXX's ground and has now moved to XX. He uses an alias. This information has been passed to 4 AMIP...

This makes it clear that she had by now gone all in on the younger Delroy Grant from south London, his being the CRO number that she quoted. She says she had spoken to his local CID at the address shown for him and that they had told her he had moved, but they didn't know where. Another assumption, reasonable but again unchecked, was made that he must have moved to Brockley Mews. Hence, despite the fact that nobody had seen or spoken to him, the Delroy Grant who lived at Brockley Mews was now assumed to be the younger man whose DNA had been taken and was on the national database. Of course, we now knew that she had plumped for the wrong one.

This was to matter a great deal, but needed a further combination of circumstances, illogical reasoning and bad communication to have its full devastating effect. The DC at Minstead, on 13 July 1999, created a nominal N253 in the HOLMES database, using all the personal details of the younger, London-based Delroy Grant but listing his home address as Brockley Mews. He was also allocated two actions (i.e. investigative tasks to be carried out). Action number A151 requested that he should:

> *TIE* [Trace, implicate or eliminate] *N253 as Minstead suspect and establish if he is the owner of BMW MV – see CRIS at Bromley for full details.*

While A152 asked him to:

> *Fully research CRIS re Burg [at Bromley]. Complete victim proforma and liaise [with Bromley officer] re forensic and progress.*

The Burglary Squad supervisor, a detective sergeant, clearly noted the CRIS report on 29 July to the effect that he had spoken with the Minstead DC and agreed that the Bromley Burglary Squad would maintain primacy and be responsible for the investigation. A week later the Minstead DC reported on action A151, saying that he had carried out enquiries into nominal N253. As the London-based Delroy Grant he was looking at had recently been arrested – and since the late 1990s DNA samples were routinely taken from prisoners – his DNA profile was stored on the national database. So, it had been a simple act to have that compared with the crime-scene samples, with the inevitable outcome that, since the profiles did not match (how could they as they each came from a different man?), Delroy Grant was eliminated – he could not be the Night Stalker. The Minstead DC followed this up a few days later with the result for action A152:

> *The only similarity between this crime and the Minstead series is that the victim is elderly and the crime occurred during the night. Victim was not disturbed. Suspect vehicle seen at time of offence but the registered keeper is not a DNA match with suspect...*

The die was now very nearly cast – N253, Delroy Grant of Brockley Mews, was deemed not to be the Night Stalker, the burglary he had committed in Bromley was deemed not to be a Minstead offence, and the golden opportunity to end his reign of terror had been missed. But surely there still should have been a chance?

Because, irrespective of Minstead, there was still an outstanding burglary at Bromley, with a good suspect whose name and address was known. It should not have mattered that he had been erroneously attributed to the wrong criminal record and DNA profile. Bromley Burglary Squad, surely, would arrest him for their crime, during which process his DNA would be sampled, his true identity established and, most important of all, a match with the Minstead scenes would be churned out of the computer?

However, despite the entry on the CRIS report by her supervisor, the Bromley officer maintained that she believed that Operation Minstead had taken over the investigation. She therefore did not carry out the usual investigative tasks one would expect – for example, no statement was taken from, or liaison maintained with, the victim, no further local enquiries were made and no attempt made to interview Delroy Grant at Brockley Mews. The Bromley burglary case was, inexcusably, simply not investigated any further.

Confusingly, although it is a matter of the clearest record that Operation Minstead had not assumed responsibility for the investigation, its DC did go to Brockley Mews, not as part of his work on actions A151 and A152 but a few weeks later, at the end of August. He later said he did this, he thought, on behalf of the Bromley officer. She said she was unaware of it though, so it is not easy to understand why he was maintaining his interest and continuing to spend time on the case. He said had seen a black woman at the address and that although the BMW was not there, she had produced to him a registration document showing ownership of the car at that address. He shared that information with Bromley and said that his expectation was, thereafter, that they would arrest Delroy Grant. He had no further interest in the man because the (erroneous) DNA elimination meant he was of no interest to Minstead. Of course, subsequent events tell us just how that false elimination came about.

After Grant's trial had completed, the 1999 debacle was investigated by the Independent Police Complaints Commission. In his evidence to that investigation the Minstead DC concluded that following his visit to Brockley Mews:

We [the police] could have arrested him [Delroy Easton Grant] for this burglary. We should have arrested him for this burglary. There is no reason that I can give why he was not straightforwardly arrested one morning and interviewed because what I said to you earlier is once a car is registered to that address and it was confirmed as being there everything else would just follow. Once you've arrested him or interviewed him or invited him in... as soon as you get him into a police station, alarm bells must ring. Was that my responsibility? I would say not.

The result of the investigation was that three officers were found guilty of misconduct in failing to be diligent in their investigation of the burglary. One had retired in the meantime but the others were given formal advice. At the conclusion of their investigation, the IPCC Commissioner for London, Deborah Glass, summed it up thus:

Delroy Grant's terrible crimes targeted some of society's most vulnerable individuals leaving them and their loved ones heavily traumatised.

The IPCC investigated the police's response to one crime linked to Operation Minstead in 1999.

It is clear that a simple misunderstanding had horrific consequences. Police missed the opportunity because confusion led to the wrong man's DNA being compared.

This mistake set off a chain of events that was compounded by poor communications between, and within, the two teams meaning that basic enquiries, such as arresting Grant and searching his property, were not done.

Had an officer from either team done this then Grant

*may have been charged for the Bromley burglary, leading
to his DNA being matched to the Minstead crimes.*

*While our investigation identified poor communi-
cation and basic policing errors, in which each team
believed that the other was responsible, we also have to
recognise that we have required officers to account for
actions taken twelve years ago, and accept that they
could not have foreseen the consequences.*

The IPCC and its successor, the Independent Office for Police
Conduct, has many critics and I have been vocal in joining them.
On this occasion though Ms Glass was absolutely accurate.

Quite starkly, the truth is that Grant should have been
arrested in 1999 and scores of victims spared their ordeal.

Chapter 22

WHO WAS THE REAL DELROY GRANT?

Delroy Easton Grant was born in Kingston, Jamaica on 3 September 1957. He was therefore thirty-five at the time of the 'first' Minstead offence in 1992 and fifty-two when arrested in November 2009. He was born into a poor family. His parents split while he was still very young, his father George having discovered that his mother Vida had been unfaithful and was in a relationship with another man. Vida's life took off in a new direction, ultimately resulting in her emigration to the USA. As Delroy grew up he knew nothing of his mother and there was never any attempt by either party to contact the other.

George then met and married Ruby, but shortly afterwards joined many of his generation of Jamaicans in boarding the boat for England. Ruby remained in Kingston, the ostensible carer not just for Delroy but also for two other sons of George from two other relationships. The reality though was that Delroy was almost entirely brought up by his paternal grandmother, Blanche, in a rural community a few miles to the west of the island's capital. Of course, the fact that she would have been the only maternal figure Delroy could remember during his formative years was seized upon by psychologists, both amateur and professional, as explaining the origins of his sexual tastes. Who knows if there is something in that – what is certain is that this childcare arrangement was common in the West Indies at the time and yet most individuals concerned seem to have grown up without a tendency to gerontophilia (sexual attraction to the elderly).

George had secured employment on the railway and was sensible enough to save money towards a home of his own, as well as sending some back regularly to his mother to help her feed and clothe the young Delroy. By the time Delroy reached adolescence he had become too difficult and wayward for his ageing grandmother to handle. George and Ruby, who'd by then joined him, had managed to get a mortgage and buy a small house in East Dulwich and so the fifteen-year-old Delroy followed his father's path and was reunited with him in south-east London. He took a place at the local comprehensive school, leaving with no qualifications as soon as he reached the requisite age. As was sadly common, while his father and step-mother brought their Jamaican culture of strict upbringing and active participation in the church with them, Delroy rebelled, finding their attempts to impose discipline restrictive. He was a young man in the big city and wanted to explore it, to be part of it.

Working at a garage, he had frequent rows with employer as well as his father. His criminal career began not with sexual or violent offences but arrests for stealing cars in 1975 and 1976, escalating to taking part in a robbery while possessing an imitation handgun in 1980. He had all too easily fallen in with a bad crowd at his local pub and tagged along with them, so he maintained, on the robbery. For his troubles he received nothing but a two-year prison sentence.

After his release he turned his hand to slightly more cerebral thievery: cheque fraud and deception. With a bit of criminal damage and carrying a weapon thrown in, his final convictions prior to the Minstead series were for dishonestly handling stolen goods. Crucially, the period of his offending ended before DNA samples were routinely taken from all offenders and so while his fingerprints were on file, his DNA profile was not. It is worth noting too that there was no hint of a sexual offence anywhere in his criminal history.

Not that his personal life showed such celibacy. Fit, good-looking and a charmer to boot, Delroy had no difficulty in attracting attention from the opposite sex and he had many relationships with many different women. However, he never really mastered the art of fidelity and also regularly found it difficult to control his temper. While to his friends in the pub, clubs and cricket team Delroy was a 'lovely bloke' and always fun to be with (as we were told repeatedly by his acquaintances after his arrest) the reality of life inside a relationship with him was different, tinged always with the threat of unfaithfulness and the pain of physical abuse when his behaviour was questioned. He married Janet Watson in Lewisham towards the end of 1975, the marriage destined to last less than four years. It bore the hallmark infidelities and violence of his relationships and, much later, was to be the bedrock of his incredibly conceived defence to the Minstead charges.

When Janet spoke to us of their relationship both the

words she used and the progression they outlined echoed to me what so many women had told me about Levi Bellfield. Charming, gentle, considerate, fun – romantic even – at the start. But once the relationship was established these traits were replaced with irritability, control, violence and infidelity. Another remark had a parallel with the Bellfield case – Janet said that such was Delroy's ego he would be loving all the attention and notoriety, even if it was because he had been discovered as a horrible predator.

It was a new relationship that took Grant from London to Leicestershire in the early 1990s, where he was again convicted of dishonesty and sentenced to perform community service. He elected to work in a care home for the elderly – just a year before official 'offence one' but as we now know, almost certainly after he had started his burgling and indecency offences against elderly women. How much did his then-undiscovered predilections influence his choice? It is certainly a reasonable assumption that it was during this 200-hour stint as an unpaid carer that he learned how to lift the infirm painlessly and safely, and perhaps acquired his habit of checking pulses, which he carried forward into his later home invasions. These are certainly not skills he would have picked up during his only other known previous employments as a DJ, decorator or driver of minicabs and delivery vans. Hugely ironic, is it not, that the sentence of a court unwittingly assisted his later atrocities?

In 1991 Grant was again at the Lewisham Registry Office, this time to marry Jennifer Edwards. Considerably younger and slightly taller than him, she was universally regarded as quite beautiful. Jennifer was a committed and active Jehovah's Witness and before long, Delroy had begun to join in with the local Kingdom Hall's activities, not only in services but helping out in their frequent days on the streets, knocking on doors, spreading the word and seeking converts.

As with his previous partners, Grant was extremely particular about cleanliness and tidiness in the home. Janet, his first wife, told of how he would go 'berserk' if he found the tiniest trace of dirt or dust. Soon this became a frequent source of friction with his second wife – on many occasions he complained to Jennifer that her housework was simply not good enough. The officers on the Minstead team found this interesting: one of the characteristics we had assumed the Night Stalker would possess was an obsessive tidiness, based entirely on his peculiar habit of carefully moving and placing items when forcing entry into targeted homes. We always said that when we finally got him we expected the search of his home address to be quite an easy and pleasant experience, so clean and tidy was it bound to be. When that long-awaited day came, we found that we had been hopelessly wide of the mark. The terraced townhouse in Brockley Mews, a new-build street shoe-horned in between Honor Oak Crematorium and the railway embankment – a private house rented for the Grants by the local authority – was an utter tip, a filthy, cluttered and disorganised tip.

Sadly, Jennifer had, not long after their marriage, been diagnosed with multiple sclerosis. Hers was the nastier, progressive form of that terrible affliction, meaning that she had no remission and the failure of the nerves within her body spread relentlessly, rendering limbs useless as it did so. With help from the local authority, the ground-floor garage integral to the house was converted into a bedroom for Jennifer. When we went there, we found various slings, pullies and grab handles mounted around her bed; not that they were of much use to her personally as she by then had no use of her legs and very little of her arms. Such was her condition that she obviously needed and qualified for full-time care. Her carer, officially, was her husband Delroy Grant – at the time of his arrest he was being paid £185 a week by Southwark Council to perform that role. In a normal couple this would have of course been ideal – a husband spending all his time caring for the woman he loved and being paid for having given up the opportunity to seek work elsewhere to enable it.

But, as we know, they were far from a normal couple; at least Delroy Grant was far from a normal husband. Not only did he use the opportunity afforded by his wife's infirmity to engage upon long-term affairs – such as the one we were later to discover he had been conducting for some time with a lady in Sydenham – but he was able to spend nights out with impunity, since Jennifer was in no position either to complain or to leave. She might well have assumed he was out with a woman, and on many nights he almost certainly was. But she did not know – could not have known – that so often that was a woman he did not know, had never met and who was being terrorised by him in her own bedroom. The icing on the cake, as it were, was that Jennifer's condition gave her access to the Motability scheme, whereby a heavily subsidised car was available in order to assist in her mobility. So Delroy even had a nice new, reliable, subsidised means of transport in which to prowl the streets looking for his victims. A car which also gave an air of respectability, since, driven carefully and conservatively, a shiny new Vauxhall Zafira is bound to attract less attention from patrolling police officers than something older, noisier or more flashy. It was an ordinary suburban family car, the perfect vehicle in which to hunt, unnoticed, around suburbia.

Perhaps Jennifer's health and mobility issues meant that Grant found it easy to conceal his secret life from her. But it was not just her – nobody who knew him believed it could be true. There was a marked difference for me in how his friends and some family reacted when compared with those of Levi Bellfield. Whereas those who knew the serial killer generally said that they knew he was bad, knew that he was a psychopath and expected that one day he would be found out, Grant's acquaintances were genuinely shocked. No, not Delroy, the cricketer, the angler, the genial neighbour, the devoted husband. More than a few times they asked us if we were sure, genuinely fearing we had made a terrible mistake and must have got the wrong man. Thank goodness, again, for DNA. Many though did tell us about his missing front teeth and reinforced what a sensible decision Grant had made to take such great pains to conceal his mouth from his victims. I think we can be fairly certain that if just one of them had added that to their description then publicity would have put Delroy on our radar very quickly.

I will not even try to unpick the many issues the case and the man might have raised with psychologists (which principally seem to be: was it about sex, about control, about the thrill?). Nevertheless, some questions remain for me, even viewing the case as a mere investigator. Grant's first conviction for burglary was in 2011, after the Minstead trial. But I know that burglary, like any other 'trade', is one that must be learnt. To enter so many houses so easily, so skilfully, he must have practised. And that suggests that there must have been unsuccessful attempts of which we were unaware. For many years, having to go back over handwritten crime reports meant any attempt by police to search for them was a complete non-starter – the resources to be dedicated to it for a proper analysis would have vastly outweighed the benefits, if indeed there would have been any benefit aside from satisfying a professional curiosity.

The other great unknown is why Grant's offending was as sporadic as the recorded offences suggest. We were able, after his arrest, to check, and there was no period of incarceration or of being abroad that affected his ability to offend, so why did he have mini-sprees followed by periods of little or no activity? Was this to do with events and activities in his personal life? Put bluntly, did he offend more when he was depressed or otherwise troubled? Did offences coincide with his either beginning or ending relationships? It proved impossible to get reliable information on all these factors; quite simply, the only person who might really be able to tell us is Delroy himself. I found out only recently (early 2020) that the indubitably inquisitive DI Nathan Eason in fact visited Grant in prison some time after his conviction, hoping to get some answers both to the scale of his offending and perhaps even his motivation. Delroy told him, summarily, to 'Fuck off!'

Chapter 23

HOW WILL THE MET PLAY IT?

In the weeks immediately following the charges being laid against Grant there was a flurry of 'Gold Group' meetings at Scotland Yard. Most of these were chaired by Deputy Assistant Commissioner Sue Akers, whom I had found very supportive during my time on Minstead. She was of course co-chair of the Force Tasking Group who had sanctioned the surveillance operation and so I guess both a little invested in, as well as somewhat pleased by, its success. Simon Morgan had, quite sensibly, been invited back into the fold – his knowledge of the historical timeline of events and how the operation had been led before I took over was likely to be of great importance as we all wrestled with what to do next. I sensed a degree of tension between him and Sue Akers; I didn't know if my perception was accurate nor what the source of the friction might be. However, it was clear that her habit of always referring to the so-called 'Frying Squad' trip to Trinidad during our meetings as 'The Caribbean Adventure' did nothing to disabuse me of my feeling.

One such Gold Group meeting focussed on media relations – how we were going to brief the papers and broadcasters before, during and after the trial. As well as Simon Morgan and I, the meeting was attended by Commander Simon Foy, a press officer named Kate Campbell who had dealt with Operation Minstead from its early days, and a consultant, a former journalist called John Steele. I knew John from his time as crime correspondent for the *Daily Telegraph*. He had been in that post throughout the Levi Bellfield investigation but had left the paper in early 2008, about the time when its management decided to reinvent the title as something more akin to a broadsheet *Daily Mail*, and that veterans such as John needed to be replaced by a younger generation. He was now consulting for police forces and, knowing his pragmatic approach, I was glad to see him as part of our team, if only temporarily.

And it was John Steele who first spoke after DAC Akers had posed the initial question, 'How are we going to play this, then?'

The former reporter was forthright in his response: 'Well, if we let Colin spin it like he did the Bellfield case then I am sure everything will be OK.'

I felt half a dozen pairs of eyes on me. I knew what John meant but felt I needed to clarify it.

'I don't agree with the word "spin", John, but otherwise I think you are right.'

I went on to tell the meeting what I had learned in the Bellfield case. Yes, in that case as in Minstead, there were skeletons in the Met cupboard. One had been serious enough that it was clear – had the mistake not been made Bellfield could have been intercepted earlier and subsequent offences prevented.

That was a situation that had absolutely been repeated here in the Minstead case.

Our approach in Bellfield had been this. Yes, mistakes had been made, but the truth was that there were numerous instances of brilliant police work thereafter. And the suspect himself, what we knew and found out about him, was so complex and so interesting a character that a paper could run his story for days. In a world of shrinking newsrooms and reducing budgets, the media had far less opportunity to chase stories than had once been the case. So, by accentuating the positive, essentially spoon-feeding them by giving access to the detail of the great detective work and to the atrocious nature of the perpetrator, they had their story. We were not *controlling* what the published story was, but by controlling what we released and ensuring it was the positive material we were able to *influence* it. So successful was this approach that I had been invited to present on it at the Media Relations course at the National Police College, so that other senior officers could learn from and share the good practice. That was what John Steele had been suggesting – that the good news story of the surveillance operation, together with the detail of the strange and sordid life lived by Grant, would occupy the reports of the case fully until something else came along.

There seemed to be general agreement around the table; at least there was no outright dissent voiced. When the meeting ended it seemed we had a plan and I took away an action to prepare an outline of what should be released and then liaise with John Steele and Kate Campbell to formulate a clear strategy. We agreed to meet again three weeks later to check on progress.

I spent some considerable time working out the lines and materials that I thought might be our press pack. However, the liaison with John and Kate never materialised. We weren't able, it seemed, to find a way to get together and it became clear that the next time we would be able to do so would be at the Gold Group meeting itself.

I arrived at Scotland Yard with a rucksack full of copies of my suggestions. But as the meeting convened it was obvious something was up. Kate Campbell said nothing to me besides a cursory greeting; John Steele was a little more expressive, with a downbeat frown he whispered to me that it had 'all changed'. Commander Simon Foy took the lead, announcing that the situation had been reconsidered after the last meeting and that the decision was that our strategy would be to invoke 'organisational contrition'. I naturally understood the meaning of those words but I had never heard them used in conjunction, as that exact phrase, before. But of course I knew what it meant. Rather than accentuating the positive, how the Met had come together and sustained a prolonged, wide and extremely professional operation to catch this prolific, determined and highly organised offender, it was to be a senior officer, wringing hands in front of the Yard's revolving sign, explaining how sorry we were and how we would learn. What a slap in the face that was for me and all the team who had given so much to make sure we got him.

Unsurprisingly, I was stunned. Rather than get into an outright argument I tried to respond in a measured way. I said something like, 'That's interesting, why did we change our minds?'

Commander Foy merely hesitated and mumbled that most unsatisfactory of answers, 'That's the decision.'

I knew I had lost but was reluctant to let go without making my feelings clear – as if they weren't anyway.

'I thought this meeting was for making decisions like that? And I thought we had made them, last time. What has changed?'

The Commander did not answer directly, there was no explanation, just advice that it was considered this was in the best interests of the force. It was delivered in such a patronising way that he might as well have added, 'But you wouldn't understand…'

Others have subsequently advised me that 'organisational contrition' was deployed for one main reason. Although it meant an admission of errors it enabled them to be ascribed to the Met as a whole, meaning that individuals could escape close scrutiny of their parts in these errors. While this might be fine for those individuals, I have two serious objections to it. First, for me it's a question of leadership. I believe that individuals should take responsibility for their own mistakes. I think it is what the rest of the force and, more importantly, the community, expects of its police. Second, having the force take the blame for everything transfers a piece of that blame to each and every officer or staff member carrying out their duties every day. And their jobs are incredibly difficult as they stand, without shouldering the added burden of being branded part of an ineffective organisation, no matter how contrite it might be.

It was not so much the effect of this decision that disillusioned me; it was the principle behind it. It was my realisation that the Met, the police service, the family I loved and cherished, had changed, changed in a way I found most troubling. I had always been completely useless at organisational politics – perhaps simplistically I had just wanted to do my job and make it possible for my team to do theirs. And when I cocked up I would say so, I would apologise, I would learn. I never would have wanted the whole force to apologise for me, let alone have expected it to. Somehow it was just wrong for a few officers to expect the Met to tarnish its reputation just to save a bit of damage to their own.

It was shortly after this meeting that I formally asked to be released from Minstead, to return to my murder team, on the basis that what remained now was just getting the case ready for court and that Simon Morgan was both keen and able to retake the reins. My plea was refused. I was told firmly, evidently from a very senior level, that I would remain as SIO for Minstead until the trial had completed. I pointed out that the trial was likely not to be heard until 2011 – and that my retirement date was 4 January of that year. By the time it came to trial I could be gone anyway. This cut no ice, I was to stay. And that was the moment that I decided I would retire, on that day, as soon as I had completed thirty years' service.

Chapter 24

PROFESSIONAL BOREDOM, PERSONAL TRAGEDY

Entering 2010 I had to knuckle down to the inevitability of being at Lewisham until Grant had stood trial, that had been the clear message I had received from those above me. Any faint hope of a return to the team at Putney disappeared when a new substantive DCI was assigned to the team. Previously it had been DI Andy Perrott acting up to lead; now I had been well and truly, officially, replaced. We had organised the usual farewell do, at my favourite restaurant, a Sardinian in Putney named 'Isola del Sole'. Nobody senior to me attended – which caused me no issue whatsoever – DC Gary Cunningham giving the speech with his usual wit, eloquence and great memory for detail. The line where he said I was not just 'A Governor but THE Governor' was especially touching. As well as a handy Windows notebook laptop (which they knew I wanted), the collection for a leaving gift had raised enough for an additional 'arty' black-and-white photograph of Jubilee House at night – my office window clearly discernible – beautifully framed with an engraved plate recording the dates of my tenure with the team. It was a really classy gift and one which I treasure as the final memento from the greatest time of my service.

My daily drudge began, forty-nine miles round the M25, counting off eight hours with very little to do and then forty-nine miles back again. There was of course lots of activity going on, going through the documents for disclosure, answering memos from the Crown Prosecution Service and tidying up lines of enquiry with additional statements. A crucial aspect of this was the sad but realistic observation that many of our witnesses were approaching the ends of their lives. It was therefore of vital importance that every tiny part of evidence was recorded in their statements, lest that be the only thing available to the court come the day of the trial. For me, the fact was that very little of this needed the SIO to play an active part and while I had to be there just in case, and to maintain leadership, the reality was that I felt depressingly under-employed, the occasional meeting with scientists or conference with lawyers became the highlight of my working week. That is how bad it had got!

Some relief was provided when I was asked to slot into Simon Morgan's place in the on-call superintendent's rota, he being not well enough to do so himself. This meant that every eight weeks or so and for a whole week I was on call 24/7 for homicide for the whole of London. The role was to ensure that new investigations were allocated to the appropriate team, that resourcing was in place appropriate to its classification, and that the investigation was carried out on the correct lines. While it was largely a role to be completed by phone or email, there were occasions when the gravity of what happened required my attendance.

Most notable of these was in August 2010 when the GCHQ employee Gareth Williams was found dead in a holdall in the bath of the security-service flat he occupied in Alderney Street, Pimlico. I attended the scene on the instruction of the on-call commander, with a brief to ensure that our Homicide Command maintained primacy in the investigation. I did so, having at the scene to deliberately and consciously step back and allow the SIO I had allocated to it to do her job. It was such an intriguing and obviously complex case I felt extremely jealous of her. I just wanted to get on and take hold of the reins and had to constantly remind myself that that was not my function now. The whole idea of being involved yet not really involved in new cases I found immensely frustrating. I later described it as being as like a waiter at a Michelin-starred restaurant – serving up all these sumptuous dishes and never being able to get even a little taste.

Shortly before that though I had dealt with undoubtedly the most difficult task I ever encountered – and the surprising thing was that it was off-duty, on holiday and in a foreign country. The tedium of most working days had made my approaching holiday all the more desirable and I was looking forward to it as never before. Since 2007 I had tried to find time do some sort of road-trip holiday in my old classic Mini with my son, Joe. The first year we had been to the International Mini Meeting in Roskilde, Denmark, but the following two years we had been part of a large fleet of old and new Minis on a trip to the Nürburgring race track in Germany. The August 2010 adventure was the most optimistic yet. I had a new BMW Mini Cooper S as well as my classic. Joe had not yet passed his driving test but by enlisting my friends Chris Wortley and

Mick Regan it was possible to take both cars. Chris and Mick were in the classic while I was joined in the Cooper S by Joe and his best friend Dan – both of whom, coincidentally, are now serving Met police officers.

Part of the spectacular plan was to set up a mobile disco in the campsite for the Saturday night, always the party night of the trip. Chris being a mobile DJ had access to the kit and we managed to get a couple of speakers, an amplifier, a mixer and some lights in the restricted space around the camping equipment in both cars. Hooked up to the electricity and protected from the weather by two large gazebos, our impromptu nightclub was complete and attracted a very diverse and international crowd from across the site. At its height there must have been more than two hundred people in our field, sharing drinks, food and jokes as we danced the night away, carefree.

I think I was the last man standing, certainly it was nearly 5.30 am before I turned in to my tent; my ultimate recollection was that I had been tunelessly belting out songs from *Jesus Christ Superstar* with an equally merry Dutch music teacher called Ellen – my recollection of the lyrics from performing it at school had survived but it was clear my singing voice had not. Later that morning I rose again at about 10.30 am and found Gordon Fletcher, the unofficial cook, planner, general leader and organiser of our group cooking breakfast on a gas stove. His first greeting was to ask me if I had seen John. He meant John Fleming, a 22-year-old member of the group who had travelled with his older brother Will and Will's wife Robin. I said that I had not, that I knew John was rather the worse for wear at about 3 am and I believed he had gone to bed then.

I then noticed Will and Robin sitting at a table that had

been re-erected among the disco detritus. They looked glum. They had all been sleeping in a large tent with two separate compartments inside, Will and Robin in one and John and Gordon in the other. When they got up they not only realised that John was not there but also that his jacket and shoes were in the tent's vestibule but Robin's were missing. I tried to push the lack of sleep and emerging hangover to one side and switch from holiday to detective mode. The logical answer would be that John had, during the night, got up and left the tent, for some reason taking Robin's jacket and trainers instead of his own. But why, when? And where was he now?

The whole group gradually assembled around the table, some with sore heads that needed to get thinking clearly. I was trying not to frighten everyone, especially Will and Robin, unduly but already my sense was not good. The consensus view was, like mine, that John had gone to bed around 3 am. Those who knew him better said that he liked a good time so much that they would not put it past him to have heard some music elsewhere and to have decided to up and find it. I thought this was unlikely, pointing out that when I went to bed at 5.30 am all else was quiet. Breakfast was served and eaten in virtual silence, everyone hoping that having just gone for a stroll John would soon appear in the gazebo berating us for starting to eat without him.

As much as that was the hope it never happened. By the late afternoon I took Gordon and Will up to the small police station near the Nürburgring circuit complex. Both my profession and my speaking reasonably fluent German of course made me ideal for the job. But my European colleagues could not help – they told us no Englishman had been arrested and, making a couple of calls there and then, confirmed that neither local hospital had seen our friend either. We returned to the campsite and enlisted the help of some fellow campers for a search, with me working as best I could to allocate areas to pairs from the very rough and scale-less map given to residents by the site owners. It was approaching 6 pm and still there was no trace.

A couple of young men had decided to go to the main police station in the nearest town, Adenau. I was unaware of this until they returned, explaining that the police had told them the policy was they would not take a report of a missing adult until forty-eight hours had elapsed. I know this is a common misconception of the police in the UK, but our police have no such rule. Always the decision is made on an assessment of the circumstances and the risk that is judged. I knew not whether it was really the German policy but considered that if I could talk to them, cop to cop, and explain my fears maybe I could persuade them otherwise.

I introduced myself to the officer on the desk, producing my warrant card and explaining that I was a British murder detective. As is often the case, Germans are at first surprised to hear a Brit speaking their language with confidence; they are then I think somehow more disposed to help, even if they themselves continue the conversation in their (usually very good) English. The officer invited me in and I got to speak with an officer of some rank, judging by the many various shapes of woven wire insignia adorning his smart green uniform. He got a plain-clothes officer to join us and I explained the situation, what I knew and what I feared. He thought for just a second, nodded to his colleague and said, 'OK, we search now.'

Driving the few miles back to the campsite we saw a distress flare being sent up into the darkening evening sky. By the time we were there, the first of the local Feuerwehr, the volunteer-retained fire service, had arrived. It seems they are the go-to service for searching rural land in the area and their speedy response, as well as that of the police, was much appreciated. They did what they could until the light deserted completely and then their leader came and told me they would be back to continue at first light.

It was a very sad evening at the camp, the jollity of Saturday night just a memory as the reality became more grim with each passing minute. By now the whole British contingent of around seventy was aware of John's absence and their well-intentioned frequent enquiries over in our corner of the field did nothing to lift our mood. The additional difficulty was that we were all due to leave for home first thing in the morning; obviously, that was going to be impossible for Will and Robin until things were somehow resolved.

As the camp broke and a dozen green VW minibuses full of police arrived, we hatched our plan to cope. Gordon and I would stay with Will and Robin, Chris and Mick each driving one of my cars home and taking Joe and Dan. I could then eventually return with Gordon in his car. Again, it was thought that my knowledge and my language skills would be useful, and in truth I wanted to stay to help. I was fully in work mode now really, trying desperately to keep my friends' spirits up while preparing them for the worst. As I was due back at work on Tuesday, I rang Hamish Campbell and explained what was going on. In a wonderfully practical and compassionate decision he told me that I was acting as a police officer assisting British nationals abroad, that I should consider myself on duty since Sunday (so I would get the leave days back) and that I should use my Met-supplied mobile phone for everything so as to avoid personal roaming costs.

It was when the helicopter which had been assisting the search flew away that I thought something was up. Then I saw the officers returning to the buses. Either they had been called elsewhere (most unlikely) or there was no need for them to search any further. The latter being my bet, I quickly distanced myself from Will and Robin and sought out the detective who had been in charge, a man of advanced years, so much so that he quite unusually had not a word of English. He told me that a body of a young man had been found floating at the surface of a large pond just yards behind where our tents were pitched. From his description it was obviously John and our worst fears had been realised.

The detective's young assistant asked if I wanted them to break the news to Will and Robin, obviously implicitly asking if I would rather do it. Unhesitatingly I said I wanted to. As I took a hundred heavy paces back towards them I could see their agonised stares, both directed to my face. I had delivered 'death messages', as they are known, countless times over the years, especially as a uniformed officer. I had spent the last ten years dealing with death and the recently bereaved virtually every working day. None of that had prepared me for what I now had to do: to tell two friends that their loved one had been taken just twenty-two years into his vibrant, joyous and promising life.

Will and Robin, I am sure, knew what was coming – but they still had to hear it before it had its full effect. Will was holding Robin tightly around her waist; as I arrived it turned into a group hug, the three of us entwined and sobbing as I somehow dragged the words from the back of my throat. Whatever the boss had said, whatever my actual function, at that point I was no policeman on duty. I was just an ordinary, wretched human being, grieving the loss of a friend with those who loved him.

Having sat Will and Robin down and ensured they had a supply of cigarettes, I jerked myself out of the sorrow again and went and told the police that they could not ask the couple to do the formal identification and that I would do it. John had been removed to the local hospital's mortuary and Gordon volunteered to accompany me there, support which I really appreciated.

When we got there, John was peacefully lying, fully clothed, his spectacles still in place. Unexpectedly, the senior detective threw me a set of nitrile gloves. I caught them and asked what they were for.

'You are a murder detective, let's examine the body,' he said in deliberately slow and well-pronounced German, ensuring I could understand.

'In England we have doctors to do that for us,' I countered, while donning the protection to show I was nevertheless up for assisting.

In hindsight it was a good decision. I was thereafter able to assure John's family that there was definitely no injury or anything else to suggest it had been anything but a tragic accident. I, somebody they knew and trusted, had seen it for myself. How much better that might be for them, I thought at the time, than having to rely on a translated official report. What I also noticed was that the button fly on his jeans was open. The logical, horrible and devastatingly simple explanation would seem to be that he had got up, grabbing the first jacket and shoes to hand, wandered the few steps to the pond to relieve himself and simply slipped in.

As we were about to depart on the most sombre of journeys home, Will said to me that it was a shame there were no fences around the pond. I remarked that while it was of course true, if it were not for the German way of leaving much responsibility to the individual then we would not have been at the Nürburgring in the first place. Allowing the general public in their road cars to use a narrow thirteen-mile race circuit – which was removed from the Grand Prix roster for being too dangerous – at unlimited speed was perhaps another manifestation of their thinking. And despite how we both would have given anything to change what had happened, in truth I think I prefer the German way.

This all meant that my final appearance at a court as a police officer, later that year, was not to be in the majestic surroundings of the Old Bailey but at the much more tranquil magistrates' court in Alton in Hampshire, at John's inquest. It also gave me a bond with a family that, no matter how infrequently we might meet, will always be there; the memory of that bitter moment in a sunny field in the Eifel forest will never leave any of us. I will always be glad I was there for them.

And much more personally, it made me realise that, despite all I had seen and done and heard and smelt over thirty years, there was still an ordinary human being with human feelings underneath. The Met might have made me, it might have shaped me and hardened me, but it had not taken me over completely. Which somehow made my decision to retire a few months later, and the prospect of living a more normal life beyond that, seem less scary and more appealing.

Chapter 25

ANOTHER MISSED OPPORTUNITY

During our preparation of the case for trial and while we were disclosing documents for the defence, another serious error came to light. It began in March 2003 and was effectively repeated several times, the last being as late in the whole sorry saga as February 2008. This all arose from the Minstead burglary which took place on 7 March 2003, and which I have detailed in full previously. However, to save referring back, I'll repeat the outline here.

The 78-year-old female victim lived in a terraced house in Lyall Avenue, Sydenham. On 7 March 2003 she went to bed at about 11 pm. She awoke at 2 am, when she got up and decided to go and make tea. While she was doing this the landing light went off, plunging her into darkness. She thought that there had been a power cut and so went downstairs to investigate her fuse box. In the hall she was terrified to see a 'huge black figure looming over her'. The intruder pushed her to the ground, got on top of her and put his hand over her mouth. She felt the thick woollen material on her face, not gloves but something like a scarf. She was worried he was going to try to suffocate her and so bravely she tried to fight him off. He tried to push the fabric in her mouth but she resisted. She managed to ask him what he wanted and he replied, simply, 'Money.' She told him she had not got much money but that what she had was in her handbag by the table – and that he was welcome to take it all, but 'Please, please do not hurt me.'

He opened the handbag and emptied the contents on to the floor. She asked the burglar to help her to get up and, to her surprise, he did, even passing her her walking stick.

Feeling somehow that he was not going to kill her, she asked if she could sit down and the intruder courteously opened the living room door for her, allowing her to sit down while he searched the rest of her house for loot. While he was doing so, he would periodically return to see her, shining his torch through the open living room door, checking she was still in the chair. On one such occasion he returned with a cloth that he used to wipe all over her hands and fingernails, presumably (and in the event, ironically) to remove any trace of his DNA or hair she might have picked up in their struggle. She then asked to go upstairs and he allowed her to do so. She sat in a chair in the bedroom and tried to close the door. She saw that her jewellery drawer had been tipped on the bed and several drawers were open, her bedroom, her private and personal space, had been ransacked. She shouted out, pleading for him to put the light on.

There was no reply, so cautiously, not wanting to anger the burglar again but desperate to see, she crept downstairs. She went to the fuse box and turned the power back on. With the benefit of light she was able to notice that the telephone and the extension ringer had been disconnected, so she went to her neighbour's house to call for the police, who arrived within minutes, shortly after 3.20 am.

After she told police what had happened, they called a doctor, and later that day he took scrapings from under her fingernails – a standard practice where there has been contact between victim and offender. For reasons I could not actually determine – but which I suspect were almost certainly a shortage of resources and the overwhelming level of demand on the team at that time – the result of the analysis of these swabs was not acted upon by the team until more than two and a half years later, in October 2005. Despite the burglar's careful and deliberate wiping, DNA matching the unknown profile of the Night Stalker was found; during her gutsy resistance the victim must have scratched him and unknowingly collected some of his skin cells beneath her fingernails.

Now knowing that this was definitely a linked offence, the then SIO, Simon Morgan, decided he should go with the family liaison officer to tell the victim in person. This was typical of his victim-focussed approach – he knew the fact that she was a confirmed Minstead victim might cause her some distress and he wanted to be there to do what he could to allay her fears and care for her.

While they were there, they found that the lady was made of stern stuff and indeed did not seem unduly concerned by her elevation to the status of confirmed Minstead victim. Over tea, and generally discussing the suspect, she was firm in her belief that he was a black man. She then added that she did not know many black men, but that the only ones she could think of she did know, and who might be worth looking at, were those drivers at the local minicab firm, Palace Cars, who used to take her to hospital and the doctor's. She gave the officers details of the firm, and her comments were paraphrased and faithfully recorded, as they should have been, in the Family Liaison logbook.

Some eleven weeks later, in January 2006, this logbook was finally read in the incident room. The HOLMES staff decided her comment might be important and so it was noted as worthy of further investigation and an action created, requesting that officers should research all black men driving cabs for Palace Cars in 2003.

However, presumably again due to a lack of resources, this action was repeatedly put off as not being a priority – in fact it was postponed without further comment three times – in April, July and December 2006. In June 2007 it was looked at once more and again put off – but on this occasion some reasoning was given: the team's priorities at that time were tracing motorcyclists in the target group, reacting to names suggested as the culprit from media appeals and researching those men who had refused to be swabbed.

This confirms that it was a resourcing issue; not so much that there were no officers but that they were all busily engaged on other lines of enquiry that were deemed to be higher priorities. Knowing as I did at this point that Delroy Grant was indeed a driver at Palace Cars in 2003, I immediately thought that it would be wrong for me to apply 20/20 hindsight. But then I thought about it for a bit longer and realised that the decision to assess priorities made at the time could nevertheless be judged without that knowledge. Trying to put myself back in that office at that time, I considered the options as would have existed then, just that decision, ignoring the wider questions as to why it had taken so long for the swabs to be submitted and then for the action to be raised.

Prioritisation of those refusing to be swabbed is quite understandable. As I have stated above, it is common sense that the actual perpetrator would be unlikely to offer up his DNA, knowing it was the first step on a path leading inevitably to a life sentence. It is the first three reasons which, I feel, do not stand scrutiny.

The sources of the motorcycle lines of enquiry were easy to trace. A victim had, back in 2003, suggested that she had heard a motorbike start up soon after the Night Stalker had left her and one of the many suggestions from officers was that when victims had described a jumpsuit it might well have been motorcycle leathers. For some time, possession of a licence to ride motorcycles had been a factor in prioritising those to be swabbed; not only was it obviously still a live line of enquiry in June 2007 when the Palace Cars action was quashed, it was still mentioned in the discussions at that first meeting I had attended in May 2009.

More difficult to understand is the prioritisation of single suggestions that were the result of media appeals. While these can sometimes lead to a breakthrough, very often they are well-intentioned but wrong, and occasionally can be downright malicious. Either way, they are notoriously unreliable as a basis for a line of enquiry and, indeed, if they remain uncorroborated, very often they are followed up only when all else seems to be failing.

So the choice made seemed to have been not to try eliminating twenty or so men who were all working at the same place and whose identities and details would have been easy to ascertain, but instead have the team continue to try to get DNA swabs from a list of thousands of frequently unwilling men who had no connection to any of the victims whatsoever. The suggestion of one of the victims, a lady who had actually seen and touched the suspect, was not acted upon, while the word of one – possibly unknown – person who had phoned in to the *Crimewatch* studio or the incident room would have had a higher priority. Often solving difficult cases relies upon maximising the odds of success and recognising opportunities as they arise. So far down the swabbing rabbit hole was the investigation at this point that the chance was missed.

It is a sad fact that these sorts of investigations require decisions to be taken which, sometimes, will prove to have been the wrong choice. It is very often simply a matter of luck whether one decision would have been better than another – even though either would have been completely reasonable and defensible. This was such an occasion. However the unfortunate truth is that it in any case would have been unlikely to make a difference. Even if a list of the drivers at the cab firm had been obtained, the most obvious first step would have been to run the names through the Minstead database. And, of course, on that record Delroy Grant of Brockley Mews was shown as eliminated by DNA and so would almost certainly not have been looked at further. That error from 1999 had well and truly poisoned the database.

It was a matter of a few days after his arrest that we realised Delroy Grant did indeed drive for the Palace Cars minicab firm in 2003 – but the fact meant nothing to me then, as I had yet to find out about the scrapped Palace Cars action. The knowledge came about in a circuitous way. Some correspondence found at Grant's home address at 19 Brockley Mews suggested he was also receiving correspondence at an address in Sydenham, SE26. Our enquiries there found the sole occupier to be an attractive and well-educated lady in her forties. It was a tidy and well-appointed home and it transpired that she had a very responsible job in banking.

She told us that she had indeed had a relationship with Delroy Grant for some months in the past and that while he had never lived in her home permanently, he had spent extended periods staying there. They had eventually fallen out and she had not seen him for a long time. She had met him, she said almost in passing, because he was often her minicab driver, taking her from the station to home after late nights at work. This discovery also provided us with another answer – the glove bearing Grant's DNA recovered near the scene of a burglary in Bromley in September 2004 was identified by his erstwhile lover as one of hers from a pair she believed she had lost – but which Grant had obviously taken.

Fortunately, the officers had asked her at which firm he worked when they met – at this stage they were correctly trying to get as much information on Grant's past as was possible. The cab office was Palace Cars and this was recorded and entered into the HOLMES system, although it was to be several months until, during our review of information as part of our duty to disclose material to the defence, the connection was made and the missed opportunity uncovered.

Had the action not been written off and the drivers at Palace Cars in 2003 investigated, then Delroy Grant could and should have been identified. Of course, by the time the DNA result was actually acknowledged by the team two and a half years had passed, which might have made things more difficult, for Grant had by then ceased to work for them. However, the regulation of minicabs by Transport for London should have meant that former drivers' records were retained and he would have remained traceable.

In 2003, a DNA result could have been obtained in a matter of days. Did the practice by the team of putting all forensic result reports into a cardboard box without typing their contents or indexing them on the database have an effect and cause the delay? And, the sad truth is, we now know that after the 1999 error, Delroy Grant of 19 Brockley Mews was wrongly shown as eliminated by dint of his DNA not matching the crime-scene stains. Such was the corrosive nature of the effects of that mistake that it is by no means certain that Grant would have been caught then even if the cab firm's records had been obtained right away. It is easy to envisage a list being obtained and the first act being to compare that with names in the HOLMES database. It is perfectly reasonable to expect that would have resulted in Delroy Grant being crossed off the list before anyone got so far as approaching him – the system would have told us that he was already eliminated. The 1999 error really had polluted everything that came after it.

Chapter 26

DID HE START MUCH EARLIER?

One of the strangest discoveries in the whole case was made during trial preparation. It caused me great difficulty in trying to do the right thing and it was a twist that I never fully ironed out until some time after I had retired from the police in 2011.

It was DC Sarah Bailey who alerted me to the possible anomaly. Sarah had joined the team voluntarily and had impressed with her work ethic and attention to detail. She was a mainstay of the trial preparation and disclosure process, and importantly, I felt, had no baggage from the past investigation and would therefore perform her duties impartially. In short, I trusted her. One day in 2010 she proved that trust was justified when she came into my office with a piece of paper. She showed it to me and sat down, asking what I thought of the crime details it bore.

It was a summary of an offence that had taken place on 14 October 1987 – a full five years before the 'first' Minstead offence. An 88-year-old woman whom I will call Rose had been raped, at night, in her home in Beckenham. It was a three-bedroomed, 1930s-built house, firmly in the middle of Minstead country, and the crime had some of the distinctive features with which we were all too familiar. The rapist had held the victim's hand, felt for her pulse on her neck and given her a glass of water after the act. Entry had been through a window, objects by the window had been carefully moved to one side and a tidy search of the house made. The suspect had been described by the victim as a black man with a soft, south London accent.

I told Sarah Bailey that it looked, to me, like a definite Minstead case. I raised the question of why it had not been included in the series and her smile reminded me what a stupid question that was. We both knew there were dozens of such crimes, deemed not Minstead simply because the team had too few resources to deal with them. This one would have had an especially significant effect on the Minstead series since it would have extended its time frame by five years, potentially meaning scores of 'new' offences might be included.

The difficulty this caused us in presenting our case to the court was that we were relying to a degree on evidence of similar fact, that is, that the features of all the offences were so distinctive and so rare that it was unthinkable that they could be anything but the work of the same man. While the DNA would convict Grant of those offences where it had been found, evidence that there was somebody else committing similar offences at the same time would throw up a smokescreen for the others, which he and his defence team would almost certainly try to exploit.

I thanked Sarah for bringing it to me and told her I would

try to draw the complete file from central registry so that I could make a decision. In my mind was that we ought to put the offence to Grant at least, but that we should also probably look at any others between 1987 and 1992 so as to gain a proper understanding of the scale of his offending. I made the phone call, only to be told that the file was already 'out', having been drawn by a detective sergeant on the 'Sapphire' (sexual offences cold cases) team at Sutton Police Station.

I called the DS to ask what his interest was and received the cheery reply, 'Don't you worry about that one, guv'nor – we've got a bloke charged and awaiting trial for it.'

I was rather explosive in explaining that this was exactly what I was worrying about – another night-time burglar raping elderly ladies in their homes in south-east London. I naturally enquired who this man was and was told his name was John Joseph McGlynn.

'Er, that sounds like an Irish name?' I ventured.

'Indeed it is, guv'nor – born in County Cork I believe.'

This posed an obvious question, which I asked the DS: 'OK… er… How would you describe him?'

His reply landed like a blow to my head.

'A white male, aged fifty-eight years, six-footish, gingery-grey hair.'

'Right. Have you heard him speak? Does he have an accent?'

'Oh yes, guv'nor, I interviewed him. He has a strong Irish accent.'

I was at the point of disbelief.

'You have read the victim statement? You know she described her attacker as black and with a south London accent?'

'Yes, of course we have. But there is DNA, you see…'

239

I arranged for him to email me the principal statements in the case and the interviews he had conducted with McGlynn and prepared myself for a disturbing evening's reading.

Sadly, Rose had died many years before I looked into the case and so it was impossible to check her story. But, reading her statement, I saw she had been absolutely clear. On the evening of 14 October 1987 she had retired to bed at about 10.40 pm, only to be awoken some hours later by two black hands over her face, pressing into her and preventing her from screaming out. She could not see very much in the dark but again stressed that she saw a black man's head, describing it as large and round. He had then flung back her blankets, lifted her nightshirt, indecently assaulted and then raped her. Thereafter he had tied her ankles to the bed and handcuffed her wrists, asking where she kept her money. She told him it was in the kitchen.

Rose also mentioned that she might have seen another black man in the doorway of her bedroom while the first man was still inside the room with her. The man then left her alone, she heard the 3 am news come on the radio by her bed, which had been softly on throughout her ordeal. The man came back while she was tied up, stroking her neck and feeling her pulse. She asked him to remove the handcuffs, which he did. She lay there for another two hours, hearing the bulletins at 4 and 5 am. The rapist then returned and searched her bedroom, bringing her an unrequested glass of water. He then returned with a cloth and used it to wipe around her vagina, remarking that she felt cold and putting the blankets back over her as a consequence.

After the 6 am news bulletin Rose waited until it began to

get light, then took a pair of scissors from her bedside cabinet, freeing herself from the ankle bindings. She got up and locked the bedroom door lest the intruder was still there, dressed and went downstairs. She saw that the phone was off its hook but, in any case, found there was no dialling tone – it had been disconnected. She therefore went to a neighbour to raise the alarm. Police attended and she found that some clocks and jewellery had been stolen, and that entry had been by force through a kitchen window. The officers examined it and saw there were obvious marks where it had been jemmied with a narrow tool.

Rose was examined by a doctor, who found bruising to her body, wrists and ankles, entirely consistent with her account both of the rape and being handcuffed and bound to the bed. The usual swabs were taken from her vagina and anus and both were to prove positive for the presence of semen. What was clear from both the statement and the first report she gave to her neighbour was this: the rapist had been a black man; there might have been another black man with him but the man who spoke to her, raped her and tied her up was definitely black. Naturally I was, therefore, troubled, puzzled even, as to how a white man could be awaiting trial charged with the offences.

It seemed, unsurprisingly, that after police attended, a full scientific examination was conducted not only in the bedroom where the attack had taken place but also at the kitchen window that had been the point of entry. This had yielded some fingerprints from the glass that had been opened and the secondary double-glazing pane, which had been removed, whole. The swabs had yielded semen but, by the state of 1987 scientific knowledge,, no further identification such as DNA profiling could be achieved from them. Despite the best efforts of the local detectives, no real progress was made in the investigation. The trail had gone cold and the investigation was shelved.

By 2009, the Met's Sapphire Cold Case team was enjoying notable success in revisiting old cases of serious sexual assault, specifically by resubmitting physical exhibits for DNA analysis. Inevitably they got around to looking at the Beckenham case and a full DNA profile from a single male source was obtained from the victim's nightshirt. That profile was uploaded to the national DNA database and it found a match. John Joseph McGlynn, who had a number of previous convictions and had most recently been arrested in north-east England for credit card fraud, when his DNA had been taken and placed on to the database. Notified of the match, the Sapphire team asked for his fingerprints to be compared to those found on the window and, again, a perfect match was found.

It was to be expected then that the officers travelled to McGlynn's home in Darlington to arrest him. They took him to the local police station where he was interviewed. He chose not to have a lawyer present and was happy to explain his story to them, on the record. What they heard was an account of events that while certainly bizarre and, to most of us I am sure, distasteful, certainly possessed one redeeming feature: it was the sort of story you would never expect anybody to make up.

McGlynn said that the DNA and fingerprints most probably were his – but that there was an innocent explanation, one which he suggested began in May 1987. He said that, although he was by no means proud of it, he had a preference, a fetish even, for women who were much older than him and that most of his relationships had been with ladies at least thirty years his senior.

He described how, in May 1987 – aged thirty-five – he and a friend had one weekday afternoon visited a café called The Rookery on Streatham Common. There they had begun talking to a couple of ladies, one in her sixties and the other considerably older – the older woman was Rose. The chatting had lasted for some time and, as was McGlynn's intention, ended with an arrangement for him to go on a date with the younger woman, whom I will call Teresa. This had duly taken place, the pair got on well and started a relationship, a full, sexual relationship.

As this had developed, McGlynn found out that the older woman who had been in the café was his new girlfriend's near-neighbour. When he had been visiting Teresa's home he had, on occasion, seen and spoken to her older friend, Rose. On a couple of occasions Rose had asked McGlynn if he would help her with a few tasks around the house and he had obliged. The last time he had done this would have been, he said, around the time of the great storm of October 1987, but before it – so almost exactly the time that Rose was burgled and raped. The task that afternoon was to fix a kitchen window which was sticking and difficult to open. Once he had carried out the repair he started chatting to 88-year-old Rose who told him that she had a stiff neck. He had offered to massage it to try to ease the muscles and, in his words, 'one thing had led to another', and they had ended up having sex in Rose's bedroom. So, McGlynn protested, the entirely innocent explanation for the presence of his DNA or fingerprints on the kitchen window was his repair work, and anything in the bedroom or on Rose's body was the result of their having had consensual sex.

Chapter 27

BUT IT'S STILL ALL ABOUT THE DNA?

McGlynn's account was breath-taking, not only in its distaste-fulness but also its implausibility. Rose had married late in life, not until she was sixty, and she had then been a virgin. She had then been widowed not many years later and since then had spent her time playing word games, listening to music and was learning to speak German. She had told the police that, during her relatively short marriage, sex with her husband had been most infrequent. Was she really likely, voluntarily, to engage in a spontaneous act of casual afternoon sex with her neighbour's boyfriend? In the absence of Rose's description of the man who had raped her it would have been a pretty much an open-and-shut case – a fanciful tale invented purely to deal with the damning scientific evidence, one which no jury on earth would swallow. But there was Rose's description and it cast a serious doubt over McGlynn's guilt. She was absolutely clear in what she had said. Her attacker was a black man. The direct quotes from her statement (taken from the judge's summing-up at the conclusion of McGlynn's case) bear this out:

I was woken by two black hands over my face. The hands were pressed against my face. I could not scream. I could hardly breathe.

She described how the man had raped her, then handcuffed her wrists before asking where her money was kept, reinforcing her judgement of his ethnicity by adding:

And I can remember that at one time there was another black man who put his head around the door whilst the other man was in the [bed]room.

Rose went on outlining how the first man had returned to her in the bedroom frequently as the burglary unfolded, acceding to her requests to loosen the handcuffs. She heard the radio news reports at 3, 4 and 5 am as her lengthy ordeal developed. It was after 6 am when she decided that the men must have gone. She took a pair of nail scissors from her bedside table and cut the cords binding her ankles so she could get up and raise the alarm.

There is another telling identification passage in her statement:

The man who put his hands over my face and raped me was black, Negro-type close cut black hair and a round-ish head. I did not see or feel any rings on his hands. The problem is that it was dark all of the time and I cannot remember anything about his face. All I could see was outlines of him. He appeared to be quite tall but I cannot be sure how tall he was. The other man who just looked in once, all I can say is that he was black, Negro. He looked taller than the other man. He did not have bushy hair.

Returning to describing the first man she said:

When the man spoke he sounded as if he came from England. There was no strong accent of any kind noticeable. Everything that happened was all in the dark and all I have is an impression that they were older than teenagers but I cannot be sure.

Of course Rose's death after the crime but before the trial meant that her statement was the only evidence she could give to the court; there was no opportunity for clarification, amplification or indeed for the defence to challenge it. There was an irreconcilable mismatch: if her description was accurate the science must be wrong – or McGlynn must have been telling the truth.

I was troubled by this greatly. Not so much that this complex and shocking case caused any great difficulty in our prosecution of Grant – the scientific evidence we had against him for the charges we had laid was as compelling as any could be. My issue was that McGlynn was being prosecuted when there were, in my view, serious doubts that he had been the rapist. These doubts would, I felt sure, be accepted by a jury, and so the prosecution was bound to fail. Accordingly, and with a sense of duty and fairness, I sent my thoughts in an email to the CPS office responsible for the McGlynn case. Almost incredibly, I simply never received a reply.

It was June 2010 that I next heard about the McGlynn case – from a completely unexpected source. I received a call from a Met Police media officer, who asked me if, in light of the forthcoming trial of Delroy Grant, I would like to offer some comment on the conviction of John Joseph McGlynn. When I seemed taken aback, she explained that he had stood trial for Rose's rape and burglary at Aylesbury Crown Court and had been convicted, receiving a sentence of fourteen years' imprisonment. I was flabbergasted, not just that the prosecution had gone ahead but that a jury had convicted him. I declined to make any comment on the case and requested that the Met did not officially refer to any connection with Grant – which they did not, and the matter at least publicly, faded away.

However, the potential for an injustice stayed with me, even after I retired. During 2012 I became aware, through a journalist, that McGlynn's legal team were putting together an appeal and I had a meeting with them. Their grounds were to be that the trial gave too much weight to the DNA evidence and that the jury had been misdirected to treat Rose's evidence of the rapist's description as a mistake. This made sense to me in many ways – chiefly that it could only be by ignoring her statement that any jury could have come to a guilty verdict. At this meeting the lawyers gave me and the journalist copies of the transcripts from McGlynn's trial, meaning for the first time I could look critically at the real detail of the case – I had not had such access, strangely perhaps, when I was a serving officer.

I read every word and it became apparent that Rose had, on several occasions, met McGlynn when he had been visiting Teresa. If he had been the rapist would she not have recognised him? I was also able to discover a bit more about McGlynn's background, including the fact that one of his previous convictions was for indecent assault. That finding ended any interest in McGlynn the journalists had; perhaps slightly cynically they judged that a sex offender with a peculiar interest in elderly ladies was unlikely to gather any viewer or reader sympathy and as such the story was not one they would run with. It was going to be down to me to try to make some sense of it alone.

Looking at it again, with access to all the information, the striking similarities with Grant's modus operandi were utterly convincing. There was the removal of the glass to enter, the cutting of phone wires, the care for the victim – all distinctive Grant traits. A thought occurred to me. Could he have done it – but with McGlynn? It is rare for serial offenders like him to work with an accomplice, but not unheard of. A crucial element would be that both would have to share the same interest and desires, no matter how bizarre or perverted they might be. We know Grant was a gerontophile, and McGlynn in his defence stated he had had a relationship with an 88-year-old woman fifty-three years his senior. So there was clearly a mutual interest. By reading their statements I now learnt for the first time that both Rose and her friend Teresa had said the man with McGlynn when they first met him in the café was black. And yet McGlynn had strenuously denied this at his trial – why did he need to? It had no real bearing on his defence; if he were lying, could it be that he wanted to maintain a distance between himself and any suggestion of being in league with Grant?

Rose's evidence in her original statement was clear – the man who raped her was black. She based this not on just a fleeting glimpse but on having the man on top of her, she described his skin tone, his hands, his hair. She was certain – as certain as she was that there were two intruders in her house. If either of her descriptions were faulty it might be much more likely to be that of the second man, who she had merely glimpsed once in the dark.

Delroy Grant, by the time of his arrest, was aged fifty-three and an accomplished burglar. A 'trade' which has to be learned usually over many years and starting at a young age. Yet there is no evidence of his being involved in burglary until the Minstead series. Who taught him, and when? McGlynn in contrast was burgling as a young man, resulting in a number of convictions in the early 1970s. Was Rose's burglary and rape where he first took Grant along to show him the ropes?

Knowing Delroy Grant and the Minstead case as well as I do, I think there is a sequence of events that would fit with the evidence and explain the surprising inconsistencies in this shocking case: Delroy Grant and John McGlynn knew each other in London in the mid-1980s and discovered they had a shared attraction to elderly ladies. They were together when they 'chatted up' Teresa and Rose in the Streatham tea room in 1987. They decided, together, to break in to Rose's house, rape her and steal her property. McGlynn actually broke in and left his fingerprints on the window pane. Grant raped her but either did not ejaculate or wore a condom and hence left no DNA. McGlynn's DNA was found because he either raped her that night as well, or because his defence story of a prior relationship was in fact true – he did have a relationship with Rose and the burglary was to enable Grant to satisfy his desires.

I found that after the 1987 rape McGlynn had left London

and that his next brush with officialdom came in 1992 when he was convicted for a string of credit card offences and thefts at Leicester Crown Court. It is also known that in the early 1990s Grant too moved to Leicester, where he took up with Jane Finlay and they became involved in credit card fraud, being convicted of dishonest handling at Leicester Magistrates' Court in 1991. Is this pure coincidence, or were Grant and McGlynn back together – offending together – in Leicester at that time? Sadly, we will probably only know how true this theory might be if Grant or McGlynn do the decent thing and tell us.

A final thought… If Grant were involved in Rose's rape, it takes the start of the Minstead 'Nightstalker' series back five years. Had the case not been ignored but properly and thoroughly investigated who knows what might have been found, what links to Grant might have emerged? Was this horrific crime on the day of the Great Storm the first missed opportunity to catch Grant, to have stopped the 'Night Stalker' series before it had even really started?

Chapter 28

BUILDING UP TO THE TRIAL, RUNNING DOWN TO RETIREMENT

Apart from the occasional discoveries like those I have detailed, the trial preparation was pretty straightforward. Sam and Debbie continued to keep such victims as survived, and the families of those who did not, up to date with how things were going and the projected timescales. As well as the apparently endless loop of reading documents, marking their status for disclosure and reading another document, the team had occasional forays into more investigative tasks. As the DNA evidence was pretty conclusive, there was less of an imperative to keep on investigating 'up to the door of the court'. Despite this, if a credible opportunity arose to garner some more evidence, then it was taken.

One such opportunity in autumn 2010 came as the result of information given to an officer on a completely different team by a registered informant. It was sketchy, vague even, but it was appealing in that it could result not only in more evidence but also the chance to return some stolen items to those who had been burgled. Essentially, a pawnbroker's shop in south-east London was identified as Delroy Grant's favoured place to convert his loot into cash and it was suggested that not only would he be known to the proprietor there but that some distinctive items of jewellery were still on the premises. Since Grant's last successful burglary was nearly a year previously, I was hugely sceptical that the last part would prove to be true but nevertheless agreed that we should obtain and execute a warrant. Irrespective of the likelihood of success or our need to acquire more evidence, I was very conscious that for most of the team it was a considerable time since they had undertaken any 'proper' police work. The information to support a search warrant was certainly there and, win, lose or draw, I thought they would probably relish the change of an early morning 'spin'. The only snag was that the day on which it was, for various reasons, appropriate to conduct the search was one on which I had an early-morning medical appointment. Notwithstanding this I told Nathan he should go ahead and lead it; they really did not need me there in any case.

I arrived in the office at about 9.30 am and was told by the few staff still in the office that the search had been fruitless. Gradually the empty-handed hunters trickled back and because of a quirk in our accommodation I saw each of them as they did. My office, a windowless construction on the edge of the main office, had been used before my arrival as a bit of a store room. Upon my occupation there was no choice but for me to keep a wheeled hanging clothes rail upon which all the team had their stab-proof vests on hangers. There was simply nowhere else for them. This didn't bother me, as the team needed the protection so rarely and thus troubled me for access to them only infrequently, and the thing was up against a long wall, causing no real reduction in my space.

However, on this day all those on the search had taken the sensible precaution of wearing their 'stabbie' and so were each coming in to replace it on its hanger.

I have often been fascinated by a difference between the sexes, something you may have noticed. Men, when removing a jumper over their head, tend to grab it at either side of the neck and tug as hard as they can until the whole thing is off. Women, however, tend to have a gentler approach which apparently better maintains the shape of the garment, crossing their arms in front of them and lifting upwards gently from the bottom hem.

Some of the disrobing officers on that morning patiently undid the Velcro straps and tabs but others took the heavy protective vest over their heads to prevent disturbing the fit adjustment for the future. I had noticed that all of these had employed the method I had always observed as appropriate to their sex. So, when DC Sarah Bailey came in, as expected she crossed her arms and gripped the lower edges of the vest. As usual, Sarah was chatting to me as she did so and I watched as she took the vest upwards, still speaking, completely unaware that she had also taken hold, on both sides, of her T shirt. She carried on, oblivious that she was now talking to me, looking me in the eye with her hands above her head, standing in her bra. I do not embarrass that easily but this was a stern test.

I blurted out, 'Sarah!' rather in the way you would to a child who had dropped a swear word in front of your favourite aunt, motioning as I did so towards her torso with my eyes. She looked down, horrified, and her first reaction – perhaps understandably – was to turn and shut the office door, to which I reacted, 'No, no, just pull it back down!' I quickly added that someone else could come in at any minute and the last thing both of us needed was being captured by a colleague with her apparently undressing in my closed office.

Thankfully, both of us recovered from our equal embarrassment. Sarah, an officer who was always supportive to me and gave her very best, went on to play a vital role in the preparation of our case for court.

Although such memorable moments of levity were few and far between at that point, the mood on the team had changed considerably. Despite being in the patient and unglamorous phase of the case, the fact that we had gone from chasing our tail, with little real hope, to arrest and charge had lifted a huge black cloud. The relationships between the officers, the banter and the socialising had all increased. While there were some, possibly incorrigible long-standing members, who still did not join in, the Minstead office became a much more pleasant place to be, even if the actual work was quite dull and repetitive. After work visits to the 'One' pub, behind the police station on the corner of Myron Place became more frequent and even a couple of 'office lunches' were organised. I was pleased personally that it was during this time I really got to know some of the team and was able to understand what I had always suspected – they were, to a man and woman, skilful and utterly dedicated but were now also proud of what they had achieved.

The last notable event during my tenure as SIO was a meeting I organised at the Lambeth Forensic Laboratories, with all of the team present. If there were to be a contested trial – as we expected – then officers were going to be giving evidence. This was so that the scientists could present to the officers, in layman's terms, exactly what the science had told us and how the various findings related to each other. I appreciated that the scientific evidence was in some instances complex – not in terms of the science but the inferences which should be drawn from it. The principle was that, where there was an offence with DNA, other conclusive forensic evidence from that offence could then effectively transfer the certainty of that DNA match to other offences where there was no DNA but the other evidence was repeated. For the most part this evidence was of tool marks, the indentations made by Grant's screwdrivers as he began to force window panes or beading. But this was complicated by more than one tool having been used, sometimes at the same scene. It was crucial that everyone understood that and would be comfortable being cross-examined about it. The chances of that were, in many ways, remote but I refused to leave anything to chance.

My fiftieth birthday was in November 2010 and my retirement date just seven weeks or so later. Like most detectives on the Homicide Command, I had a considerable number of days owed to me for rest days that I had not taken. By adding those to the balance of my annual leave and factoring in the bank holidays over the Christmas and New Year period, I could almost make my birthday my last working day – which I thought might be a nice present to myself. I was in fact one day short but then remembered that there was a duty I had to complete on 10 December. That was the day I was due, along with five officers from my old team, to attend a ceremony at Scotland Yard to receive our commendations for the Bellfield investigation, which of course had been completed almost three years previously. The wheels grind slowly in the Met sometimes, even when they are praising you. Especially when they are praising you, some might say.

I thought that would work nicely. Last day on my birthday, say goodbye to the Minstead team and then return for the commendation ceremony, which would then turn into another farewell, this time to the Bellfield people. Perfect. I got the requisite forms from the administration office at Lewisham, filled them in and they were submitted. It took about three minutes; thirty years ended with a few strokes of a biro. And not once did that pen hover or pause. As much as I had loved what I had done, what I had achieved, I was certain that I could do more. What, exactly, I really did not know but I was certain I was ready.

Neville Hylton gave a little speech and the gifts at the low-key affair that was my goodbye drinks in the One. Coincidentally, Dave Edwards, who has been a friend since school right to the present day and was himself a DI with about ten months to do, was at a meeting at Lewisham that day and so came along too. I thanked them and promised them I would be OK, enjoined them to make sure Delroy Grant got convicted – and that was it. I went off to Austria to spend a week with another old schoolfriend and then came back for the commendation ceremony.

At the end of the ceremony there was a light buffet and a glass of wine. During this I was approached by Cressida Dick who, as the Assistant Commissioner had been very supportive of the Minstead operation but with whom I had not spoken for several months.

She tilted her head slightly and remarked, 'I was not aware you were retiring, Colin?'

'Yes, ma'am – after today I am out of here, never to return.'

'That's a shame, you are still young and still have a lot to offer. Why are you going?'

'Essentially because, er, well I've got pretty unhappy doing what I have been for the last year, so I thought it probably better I went.'

'Oh, you really should have said something…'

'Oh, I did ma'am. A few times.'

At which she pursed her lips and nodded, moving on to the next commendee.

Another afternoon and evening of excessive drinking and reminiscing followed, this time in the Abbey Well near Scotland Yard, just the Bellfield people, all without a senior officer coming near me. Excellent. And that was it, no fuss, no fanfare. With barely a glance over my shoulder, either physically or metaphorically, I was gone.

Chapter 29

THE TRIAL

After the usual series of pre-trial hearings, some by video link, Grant's trial was finally set to begin on 3 March 2011, just two months after I had retired. The venue was Woolwich Crown Court, useful given that Grant was on remand in the nearby HMP Belmarsh and so could be brought to court every morning through the connecting tunnel. It made little difference to me; I had no evidence to give, I was not going to be required to be a witness and, as interested in the outcome of the proceedings as I most obviously was, I assumed it was a foregone conclusion – as ever, the DNA would seal it. The prospect of trekking into London from Surrey and then changing twice to get across to Woolwich, at my own expense, every day for a few weeks was not appealing. As things proceeded, as the outrageous defence Grant was running emerged, I almost wished I had made the effort.

Following the inevitable two days of legal argument, the trial proper began before a jury of seven men and five women when the judge, Peter Rook QC, called upon our leader, Jonathan Laidlaw QC, to open the prosecution case. It was during his long and detailed exposition of the nature of the evidence and the detail of each of the twenty-nine offences for which Grant stood trial that Mr Laidlaw introduced the nature of Grant's defence. He knew of this because, slightly unusually, Grant had submitted a detailed defence statement. Although these have been a feature of criminal trials since the disclosure process was introduced by statute in 1996, commonly they said nothing of real importance, representing simply a vague denial of the offence with no real clue as to the nature of the basis of the defence. Something along the lines of 'I was not there, if I were I did not do it and if I did it, it was an accident' might be how one could sum up most of these documents. Delroy Grant's was much more expressive; this is how Mr Laidlaw described it in the opening speech:

> *In a written document provided in January of this year, the defendant has set out the defence he has decided to run. Let me introduce you to this.*
>
> *First, he denies having committed any of these offences: so not a single burglary and certainly not any of the sexual attacks. Instead, the defendant is going to say that it is he who has also been a victim in this case in a quite extraordinary attempt by his ex-wife to frame him. This is what he has come up with.*
>
> *He is going to say that his ex-wife, a lady called Mrs Janet Watson, collected and saved samples of his body fluids – so both semen and saliva – during their relationship and then, motivated by malice and in order*

to satisfy a grudge that she holds against him, she has set about this plot to implicate him.

How she would know back in 1979 that in due course the scientists – who had not even then invented the technique – would be able to recover DNA from semen and saliva is a question you might well ask. It could not, of course, have been Mrs Watson who carried out the burglaries and the rapes and the other sexual attacks: a male undoubtedly committed these.

So the elaborate plot involves Mrs Watson using another man to commit the offences, and, so the defendant will say, using a syringe to leave the defendant's semen and saliva at the scenes of these attacks.

It is, as I say, a quite extraordinary claim and, I am sorry to say, it is a further indication of what little regard this defendant has for his victims and what he has done.

There are also some rather obvious problems with this defence, which you will no doubt consider in due course. First, however badly the defendant and his ex-wife had got on and however appallingly he may have treated her during their marriage, do you think for one moment she would fix on a scheme such as this? Or is it clear to you that it is the defendant who has dreamed this story up for the purposes of this trial?

Next, the timings are rather inconvenient for the defendant. His relationship with Mrs Watson came to an end in 1979. The first offence in the series with which the defendant is charged was not committed until 1992. Is it to be suggested that she bided her time for thirteen years – carefully storing his body fluids during *this period – before persuading a male associate to begin committing these burglaries and rapes, at which he left samples of the defendant's semen as part of her scheme to get back at the defendant?*

Perhaps more to the point, no victim, in any of their accounts of what happened, makes any mention of seeing the intruder with a syringe or anything like that, and the scientists found no trace of this individual, so no third-party DNA from another male person was recovered. If there was another man raping these old ladies, why was there not a second DNA profile recovered, by way of example, from the vaginal swabs? Was this unknown man able to carry out all these offences without leaving any of his semen, saliva, etc.?

Finally, how does the 'plot by the ex-wife' account explain away, in the last in this series of offences when the links are not DNA links, the connection to the car the defendant was driving and the clothing and articles found in it.

It is, and I make no apology for saying this again, an extraordinary defence for the defendant to run, borne perhaps in part by the arrogance which characterises his offending and which makes him incapable of facing up to what he has done.

Breath-taking perhaps does not even begin to describe it. It was a fantasy defence, the like of which few if any of us had heard before. It is perhaps a testament to the power of DNA evidence: it is simply so difficult to refute, especially in those rape cases such as some of these, where there can be no question of consent being at issue and the DNA comes from samples found on internal swabs. Those unfamiliar with our legal system might wonder how something as ridiculous as this gets taken seriously by the court. The fact is that every defendant has the right to put forward a defence, and to have a legal team advise him in doing so – a team obliged to run the defence as it is put to them by their client, no matter how incredible it might be.

Grant, as expected, cut a quiet, thoughtful and polite impression in the dock, smartly dressed and occasionally donning spectacles to examine a note or document. All the evidence from victims, even those who survived, was given either by reading their statement or playing the recording of it being taken. The defence team had obviously persuaded Grant that there was absolutely nothing to be gained from parading a succession of the elderly and infirm through the court; indeed, there would be much to be lost as the sorry sight would almost certainly harden the jurors' minds to the atrocities of which he was accused. Although this was undoubtedly a huge incentive for the defence not to call the victims, their explanation for the jury was the rather more palatable suggestion that, as Grant did not deny that the offences took place – merely that he had not committed them – there was no need to test the recollection of the victims. This stance was enabled of course as none of them was able to give any useful identification evidence that specifically pointed to Grant.

The statements read by Mr Laidlaw in his luxurious voice laid bare the trauma of the victims. The recordings gave the jury the opportunity to see the victims, their pain as they recalled their ordeals, as well as the reinforcement of just how vulnerable they had been. Many of them outlined how Grant's treatment of them had changed their attitude and their lives going forward. So striking, so heart-rending are these stories that I have dedicated a separate appendix just to them.

The evidence for the prosecution was elicited with precision customary of the best lawyers examining professional witnesses. At every offence charged, either Delroy Grant's DNA had been found or, where it had not been, entry had been effected with the same tool also used at another offence where his DNA was present. So certain were the scientists, so watertight the chain of custody of the exhibits, and so heart-rending the statements of the victims, it really did appear that conviction would be a foregone conclusion – as much as any criminal trial with a jury ever can be so regarded. The case for the Crown was clear.

In a belt-and-braces pre-emptive strike, the lead DNA scientist Ray Chapman added to the evidence of DNA found at crime scenes a more general exposition of the uniqueness of an individual's DNA, addressing head-on the question of whether a child could possess the same profile as his father, and also the practical difficulties of storing body fluids for a long period and then trying to extract a reliable profile from them. Just in case, to prevent either of the daft defences apparently advanced by Grant gaining any traction with the jury. He was followed by Grant's ex-wife, Janet Watson, who not only gave detail and colour about the character of her former partner but was asked about the fantasy tale Grant had included in his defence statement. She quite understandably described it as 'unbelievable', adding that 'it's ridiculous' and at one point losing the composure she maintained virtually throughout, blurting to Grant, 'You are a liar!' The prosecution case complete, it was now time for the court to hear that defence.

It is often uncertain in high-profile cases whether the defendant himself will give evidence. There is no obligation to do so, the case is for the prosecution to prove and if the defendant feels they have not done so then it is open to him to say nothing and just let the jury make their decision on the basis of what they have already heard. Any doubt was dispelled when Courtenay Griffiths QC, Grant's illustrious leading counsel, opened the defence by calling his client. After setting the scene with a summary of his life to date, including reference to his convictions for dishonesty and his tortuous love life – during which he had fathered no fewer than eight children – he committed himself to the defence outlined in the statement, with the phrase, 'The DNA was planted by someone else. Janet Watson, with someone else.'

When pressed on this mystery accomplice he simply replied, 'An unknown person, at this time.'

The story behind the defence headline was just as ridiculous. Grant suggested that in 1979 Janet was refusing to have sex with him as she feared he would transmit to her a disease he might have picked up during his philandering. She had, he said, insisted that he provided her with a series of semen and saliva samples, which she was to give to an acquaintance who worked at Guy's Hospital, for testing. These, he maintained were the source of the DNA found at crime scenes and indeed inside rape victims. She had had somebody place the fluids there, using a syringe, in order to frame him, out of 'malice, hatred, violence maybe'. He was unable to explain why she had waited fifteen years to do so – nobody, though, thought to offer the obvious suggestion that she was probably waiting for DNA profiling to be invented.

Grant went on to explain that on the evening of his arrest he was trying, unsuccessfully, to buy some cannabis. He denied making the remark about always wearing gloves when being fingerprinted, accusing the officers of lying – just as they had been when they said he gave a false name when first stopped and when they accused him of suggesting the DNA could belong to his son. The incriminating items found in his car had been planted – not by police but by the mystery accomplice assisting Janet Watson, and his lover's glove bearing his DNA found at a crime scene in 2004 had probably been taken, he said, from her bin in order to bolster the framing job. The last allegation was described by Mr Laidlaw as 'cock and bull'.

The jury retired to consider its verdict on the afternoon of Tuesday, 22 March 2011, the summing-up of the evidence by the judge having been scrupulously fair but underlining to all those present just how powerful the case against Grant was. Many were surprised that a verdict was not forthcoming that same day; more so when on the morning of Thursday, 24 March Judge Rook had to call the jury back and give the direction that he would accept a majority verdict, that is, one on which at least ten jurors agreed. Just half an hour later they returned again, this time with a verdict and Grant was found guilty, by a majority of ten to two, on all counts.

The following morning Grant was told by the judge, 'Your depravity knows no bounds.' He recounted some of this depravity before declaring that 'your offending is in a league of its own' and sentencing him to life imprisonment, recommending that he must serve at least twenty-seven years before he would be eligible to apply for parole. Delroy Grant will therefore be in prison at least until he is eighty years old. I had never doubted that he would be convicted and so there was little of the usual relief or elation at the verdict. What was important though was that his sentence would keep him locked up until he would be too old to start offending again. That was a cause for real celebration – and relief.

One aspect of the trial troubled many. Did the two jurors who did not want to convict Grant really believe that there was doubt, that his incredible and patently invented defence could be true? The deliberations of juries are, for very good reason, something into which official research is not permitted. However, as unreliable as it might be it is worth my explaining that I subsequently heard that an officer from the Minstead team bumped into one of the jury members shortly afterwards and was told that the two reluctant jurors had said, from the very start of the trial, before a word of evidence had been heard, that their mistrust of the police and the establishment was such that they would as a matter of principle, never convict anyone of anything. Somehow, I feel relieved at this – possibly surprisingly, I would rather accept that their action was due to some sort of bigotry than that they really believed the events given in Grant's defence might have taken place.

Chapter 30

REFLECTIONS

Immediately post-trial the organisational contrition started, led by Commander Simon Foy, not in uniform by the Scotland Yard revolving sign as I had visualised, but in a smart suit outside Woolwich Crown Court. The hand-wringing and apologetic tone were just as I knew they would be though, guaranteeing that officers throughout the capital would have to answer for the mistakes made to members of the public for the next few weeks.

BBC *Crimewatch* had a 'case solved' programme listed. I tuned in more out of curiosity than anything else. I had not been approached to speak to them at all and I thought it would be interesting to see how they dealt with the surveillance operation. In the event I was shocked at the line they took. It was not just that the surveillance operation was not mentioned even in passing so much as the fact that the whole focus of the film was on DNA; it was effectively saying that it was the science that solved it. Staggered, and having just discovered Twitter, free of the restrictions of being a police officer I turned to that medium to express my frustration on 31 March 2011:

> *#crimewatch #nightstalker I do now know what de-Stalinisation was like – but at least he was dead.*

I did a number of media interviews and was, I thought, simply honest about the standard of work which I had found had gone before me. Others saw it as unfairly scathing and, looking back, I understand that. It's probably true that I let my frustration with the whole thing and the way I had felt bounced into retirement overpower a more rational train of thought. It made for good copy, but if I had the chance to do it again I think I would be more considered; the fact was that it was always a very difficult enquiry and I should have considered that more before rushing to judgement on my predecessors. I hope I've achieved that in what I have written here.

A few interesting if rather silly trivialities were thrown up by my post-trial actions though. A former officer, from long before my time on Minstead, took it upon himself to comment on as many online newspaper articles that he could find, assuring the readership that I had nothing to do with the success of the operation. Despite his hiding behind a pseudonym, he was not a particularly well-hidden troll and I managed to trace his true identity and email address on the internet fairly easily. I then, thankfully, thought better of engaging in a debate with him and just let it slide.

More amusing was the Wikipedia entry about Delroy Grant. At first it had no mention of me at all, then, such is the nature of that online do-it-yourself encyclopaedia, somebody edited it to reflect my role. They did so absolutely fairly and accurately, I thought – and demonstrated a degree of knowledge that suggested it had to be somebody from inside the operation. It was then deleted, only to be restored, deleted again and restored again many times over the next few days. It became my first and last task of every day: take look at the Wiki entry and see who was winning. I got bored of it, as I presume they did too, and I do not know who won out in the end. And I really don't care either. But it was nice to feel that there was somebody who was still batting for me.

Looking back more at the substance of the investigation, something became crystal clear to me. The poisonous effect of the 1999 mistake, that simplest of human errors where an assumption was made and never checked, had sat unseen but its hidden effect, of which we were all blissfully unaware, had significantly narrowed the opportunities for success. It had effectively blocked most of the ways in which the Night Stalker could be identified. Because once Delroy Grant of Brockley Mews, SE4, had been shown on the HOLMES database as eliminated, confirmed by his DNA not matching the Minstead scene profile, that would prove a dead-end to any enquiry that led someone on the Minstead team to search there for him.

For example, in 2001, after concerted attempts to bring the Night Stalker series to public attention, a man had called in to the incident room suggesting Delroy Grant as a possible suspect. This had properly been checked, the first step of which was to see if he were 'known to the system'. So HOLMES was checked, his status as eliminated noted on the message and it ended there and then. No further work was done, indeed was necessary, because we already knew it could not be him, the HOLMES account had told us so.

This case was an instance where it really did happen, but one can extend this principle to almost any desk-bound investigative action. Say Grant's car was seen near an offence and somebody takes the number. It is registered to the Motabilty scheme and his wife at Brockley Mews. The officer gets that information and so logically then searches on HOLMES for the address. It returns the male occupier as Delroy Grant, and he has already been eliminated by DNA. End of line of enquiry. There are many similar situations that might be envisaged – all lead to Delroy Grant not even being spoken to but instantly discounted.

This really means that the only ways he was going to be caught was if he left a fingerprint at a crime that would then be matched to those on file that he had given all those years ago, or if he were caught in the act. We strongly suspected at the time the truth was that, knowing that we had them on file, he was always going to be ultra-careful not to leave a fingerprint. But we had no way of knowing that he had, as an eliminated man, been taken out of the suspect pool for swabbing. And that, accordingly, it mattered not whether we swabbed one or one thousand men a week – we were never going to swab the Night Stalker because he simply wasn't on the list to be swabbed.

To catch him in the act needed one of two things. First, good fortune – such as the near miss on the second night of surveillance, when there was the epic foot chase in Lambeth and he was a few feet or a split-second away from being brought down by a response officer. Alternatively, he would be arrested if we were ahead of him, lying in wait, ready to pounce as he committed a crime right in front of us. By choosing to go down the proactive surveillance route, we had unwittingly taken a path that could work, unaware that not only were all the other paths not working, it was actually impossible for them to.

Some detractors pointed out the vast scale and expense of the surveillance operation, that it was so unusual, unprecedented even, and that with command of those levels of resources success was inevitable. There might be some truth in that, though I can assure them that on the days just before the arrest when there were no offences being committed and nothing but cats and foxes entertaining us on the streets of Shirley, an arrest seemed anything but inevitable to me. At times it seemed more like an impossible dream, a fantasy that would never be fulfilled.

Many have asked what the 'additional' cost of the operation was, but I have no idea, there was no way of my knowing. Beyond the normal wage, buildings and vehicle expenses that would have been incurred usually by the officers even on their normal duties, there was an additional overtime budget, but I never had to manage it so I do not know what it was. I view the idea of the cost to the organisation like this: whatever the surveillance operation cost in total over seventeen days it was probably in the hundreds of thousands at the most. There can be no doubt that for the preceding seventeen years that same overall cost was in the millions. And that the latter figure would have continued to rise every day, every week and every month that Operation Minstead continued investigating in a manner that, when all is said and done, never could have succeeded.

That would also have meant that more and more elderly people in south-east London would come to be terrorised, assaulted and stolen from by the Night Stalker. So to me it matters not whatever the surveillance operation cost. Those vulnerable victims were the important ones. It was a more than worthwhile investment.

Another issue upon which I looked back in some detail was to try to explain why the investigation had maintained its direction for so long. This was brought into sharp focus by the relative speed with which a drastic change in strategy brought success. Central to this theme I believe was the distinction between chasing a rapist and chasing a burglar who sometimes raped.

I have gone into some detail already to explain how the 'We're not a burglary squad' mantra sounded an alarm for me – and also how the team's position in the Homicide Command might have initiated and perpetuated this state of mind. But in addition, if one looks at the media releases during the investigation, the tone and content make it clear that this was a rape investigation, on some readings nothing but a rape investigation.

This extract from the influential south-east region newspaper the *News Shopper* in March 2005 is a good example:

CRIMEWATCH UK'S RECONSTRUCTION OF A SERIAL RAPIST'S ATTACKS ON ELDERLY WOMEN HAS RESULTED IN POSITIVE LEADS, SAY DETECTIVES.

Operation Minstead, the hunt for the rapist stalking Sidcup, Orpington, Beckenham, Croydon, Forest Hill and Catford, has featured on the BBC show twice before.

The *Sutton & Croydon Guardian* of the same period was no different:

> POLICE HUNTING A SERIAL RAPIST WHO PREYS
> ON ELDERLY WOMEN SAY A CRIMEWATCH
> RECONSTRUCTION HAS RESULTED IN A NUMBER OF
> POSITIVE LEADS.

And more than a year later in October 2006, as it reported what it was later to dub 'The Frying Squad' trip, the national *Daily Mail* at least tipped its hat to the burglaries, but reading the introduction to the piece gives the impression at the very least that every crime involved a rape:

> DETECTIVES FLY TO TRINIDAD IN NIGHT STALKER HUNT
> *Detectives have flown to Trinidad to make an appeal for information in the hunt for one of Britain's worst serial sex attackers, Scotland Yard said today.*
> *Police have spent more than eight years on the trail of the rapist and burglar known as the Night Stalker, who is believed to have a sexual fixation with the elderly and to be behind 98 separate crimes over 15 years.*

And the BBC, on its website in 2009, was still emphasising the sexual aspect:

> SERIAL SEX ATTACKER STRIKES AGAIN
> *A serial sex attacker and burglar responsible for more than 100 attacks on pensioners across south-east London has struck again.*

A police spokeswoman said a number of incidents in
the last month had been referred to Operation Minstead,
the unit set up to capture the suspect.

Why do I think this all mattered? Well, by characterising the
Night Stalker always as a rapist or sex attacker, the media
reinforced that trait when in reality it represented only a small
proportion of his crimes. Police media releases and internal
communications supported and maintained this stance and
so inevitably everybody – police and public alike – saw the
investigation as a hunt for a rapist. This, probably subconsciously,
dictated the strategy deployed to try to catch him.

Rape investigations are seldom solved by proactivity.
In most cases – certainly of one-off offences – it will be the
science, DNA, swabs, body fluids, injuries combined with the
witness testimony, especially from the victim, which leads to a
conviction. These are essentially reactive investigations, taking
place after the event, primarily because they are events which
might well be spontaneous but would otherwise be impossible
to foresee. This was the approach maintained by Operation
Minstead throughout most of its existence.

The few serial rapists that have been captured by proactivity
have invariably been arrested in the act or shortly after, where
the rapes were occurring in a loosely defined area of public
space. However, these cases – and there really are just a handful
of them going back forty years – involved a suspect whose
only crime was rape, where there was no alternative, and each
involved just a small number of offences in the series.

Delroy Grant had raped but he had committed many, many
more burglaries where he stopped short of that offence. Indeed,

in a significant number there was no indecency to speak of. In 2009, Delroy Grant was not primarily a rapist: he was a burglar who, actually a few years in the past, had sometimes raped the occupier. But he was at that time a prolific and active burglar, who was arrested pretty quickly once the strategy to effect it was changed – to one tried and tested for use against prolific burglars, an intelligence-led, proactive, surveillance operation aimed at catching him in the act. From my knowledge of the case at the time and looking back, I see no convincing reasons why this course of action could not have been taken during his 1999 spree – but then it would have needed the appreciation of exactly what sort of criminal was being sought.

VICTIM QUOTES

Throughout this book I have tried to convey a sense of what these offences meant to the victims. The terror of that initial encounter, of being woken up in the dark by a masked intruder, is blindingly obvious. But how could I illustrate what this meant for these people, how they then came to live out the last few years of their lives? I found myself increasingly reviewing what they had themselves said, in their victim-impact statements read to the court or, in one or two cases, to the media thereafter. And no matter how much I reworded them, whatever I came up with to summarise their feelings, I realised that their own words would always have the greatest impact. Therefore, I have selected a number of them and reproduced them below. I have added no commentary; the palpable strength of feeling and sadness recorded in them is such that there is no need.

This is a record of the way in which incredibly brave women and men tried to cope with what the depraved Delroy Grant did to them.

81-YEAR-OLD WOMAN

It is a nasty feeling to know that a stranger has been through your home... during the incident, I feared the man was going to nobble me. By that I mean I was fearful he was going to finish me off. I was in no position to defend myself due to my age and infirmity. The assault was absolutely ghastly and I want to forget about it. However, I have to live with the fear that he will return.

77-YEAR-OLD WOMAN

It is something that I shall never forget completely. It still feels so recent. I feel a huge amount of resentment and wonder how the suspect chose me. I often think to myself: why me? or why any of the other victims? I also feel a sense of indignation and anger, as I feel that I had done everything reasonable to avoid this sort of thing happening. After the incident I moved out of my house... I put my house on the market and it sold fairly quickly. I had to dispose of a lot of my furniture that belonged to my parents in the house because the police needed to do some forensic work there. I moved into my sister's house nearby. I stayed there until the police left my house. Whilst I was there, I found myself very security-conscious and locked and bolted everything. I did not want to go back to my house until it was secure.

DAUGHTER OF 82-YEAR-OLD WOMAN WITH DEMENTIA

My mother is eighty-two years old and she lives alone. She suffers from Alzheimer's disease and has done so the last four or so years… For Mum to be able to go back into her house, my brother-in-law had to make arrangements for Marion Homecare to provide someone to stay overnight with Mum every weekday for four to six weeks, while we – my sister, her husband and I – took it in turns to stay over at the weekends. The home-care person staying overnight cost extra and we had to rearrange our family commitments to stay at the weekends. This is because we were worried Mum would not settle in her house after the shock of someone breaking in. Mum did not feel secure in her home any more. Getting the windows fixed and changing the locks on the doors cost £701.50. It took five weeks for the windows to be fixed as the frame had to be made specially. Mum was very confused, anxious and insecure when she got back into her house.

87-YEAR-OLD WOMAN

Since the burglary, my memory has deteriorated considerably. It has left me feeling a bit vulnerable and on edge. I now want to leave the house I have loved so much. It can never be the same. In the New Year, I plan to sell the house, and move down to Devon. It is a shame to leave the home where I have had so many happy times and such lovely memories.

Since the burglary, I don't love the house the way I did. I can't wait to get out and go down to Devon. I feel so alone now… since the incident I feel like an old lady. Before I did not.

71-YEAR-OLD WOMAN

Before I was burgled, I was very outgoing. I used to go out and about dancing with friends all over London, mostly ballroom dancing and the odd tea dances. I'd also go out to the cinema, the theatre, lots of social dances, at all times of day or night. I drove back then… I really enjoyed my life. It shattered my feeling of being secure in my home. Immediately after this incident and indeed up until now, I do not sleep well out of the fear that I will be attacked in my home. The fear keeps me awake. Every noise upsets me. I'm very nervous at sounds that I don't recognise.

82-YEAR-OLD WOMAN

I had to undergo many tests for various infections. I then had to wait until November 1999 for HIV tests to be done and wait a couple of weeks for the results. This was very worrying because I did not know if I had contracted any infection. I couldn't go back to the house at first. I moved in with my son and his family… I couldn't live at my old home because I thought the man would come back. I did not feel safe there.

88-YEAR-OLD WOMAN

That man did awful things to me. And I still have terrible mental and psychological scars to show for it. This man has taken my life away from me. I still have nightmares about what happened. For months I was terrified he could have passed on a disease to me. I have lost my peace of mind, my home and my independence.

SON OF 86-YEAR-OLD -WOMAN

He has ruined the winter years of my mother's life.

84-YEAR-OLD WOMAN

I don't have nightmares now, but I make sure I take certain measures. I have to leave a light on, I make sure all the doors and windows are locked, even in the summer. I cannot sleep if they are open because I think he will be able to get back in.

83-YEAR-OLD WOMAN, HEARING OF GRANT'S ARREST

Thank you so much for telling me. Now I can go back to sleeping at night and being awake during the daytime.

88-YEAR-OLD MAN

I cannot emphasise enough my feelings of embarrassment and humiliation during the attack and subsequently. I feared for my life and believed I was going to be murdered.

HOW MANY DID HE COMMIT?
WHAT DID HE DO?

One of the things I am most commonly asked about this case, both by journalists and the wider public, is just how many Minstead crimes do I think Delroy Grant committed? My answer is always that while nobody can be sure, it is certainly in the hundreds rather than tens. When, after charge and before trial, we tried definitively to judge the scale of his offending we found it impossible.

The offence with McGlynn (if it were Grant, of which I am pretty much convinced) having taken place in 1987, it is reasonable to assume his offending took place over twenty-two years. But throughout that time many burglaries will have been recorded where the offender was never found and where the features were not spotted as forming part of his signature. Digital crime recording in the Met only became widespread in the second half of the 1990s, prior to that paper crime reports were filled in and these, even if they still exist and can be found, do not lend themselves easily to being searched for Minstead quirks.

The best that I can offer is an 'at least' figure, based upon all those we were able to find during trial preparation. This was a total of 204 offences, from August 1990 to November 2009. All of these were burglaries committed at the homes of elderly people. Overwhelmingly these victims were female, only twenty-five male victims were recorded. The victims were aged between fifty-eight and ninety-three; however, they tended towards the upper end of this range – more than three-quarters of them were aged over seventy.

In analysing just what these unfortunate victims endured at Grant's hands, it is important to remember that almost all of them had the terrifying experience of being woken up, while at home in their own bed and alone, by a masked intruder shining a torch in their face. Only three victims slept through and had no interaction with their intruder. In addition to that horrible experience, Grant at least 'controlled' almost all of them, his favoured methods being to hold a gloved hand over their mouth, to pin their shoulders or wrists to the bed with his hands or even to sit astride them, letting his superior body weight do the trick.

In seventy-six cases the victim reported an assault beyond this – a slap, being pushed over or in a few cases, a punch. And there were fifty-two cases where the assault was indecent, where the victim was female this usually involved touching the breasts or vagina or both. Male victims indecently assaulted reported touching of the penis or anus or both. There were just five instances of rape reported; Grant was charged with and convicted of all of these.

Four offences took place in the Surrey Police area, near the border with Greater London in that force's East Surrey division.

All the other offences were in the Met area and were confined to just five boroughs – Bromley, Croydon and Lewisham suffered the most, with just a handful of crimes reported in Southwark and Lambeth.

It can be seen from this that the characterisation of Grant as first and foremost a rapist is to over-simplify. Yes, he was a rapist; yes, he was certainly a gerontophile who took sexual satisfaction from encounters with the elderly. Essentially though he was a burglar who stole cash and jewellery – but one who frequently indecently assaulted and occasionally raped his victims.

As burglars go, he was very unusual. He had a sophistication to his crimes, to his planning and to his methods of entry that are rarely seen in volume crime offenders. Targeting a certain type of property is not that rare; burglars will often have a favourite because they find entry to them particularly easy. For Grant though there was a different motivation – the type of property he targeted would invariably deliver a victim within his desired age range. This was important for him. Certainly his desire for interaction with the occupier makes him extremely unusual since most burglars will only break in if they are sure the premises are empty and indeed usually flee if they are not.

When all the factors are taken together it drives to a conclusion that Grant was unique. He was a criminal who committed the most depraved offences, who terrorised the vulnerable, elderly population of one quarter of our capital city and yet managed to keep this double life secret from his friends, family and, of course, the authorities throughout two decades. Delroy Easton Grant was a man the like of which had not been seen before and, we must hope, will never be seen again.

29-10-2009 05:12:58

Above: The unbelievably grainy, obstructed photo from which – somehow – Andy Wooller at the Transport Research Laboratory discerned was a Vauxhall Zafira (the B model, with updated styling), and gave us a rabbit to chase.

Middle and below: The clothes worn in the photos on the previous page were found in Grant's car after he was arrested.

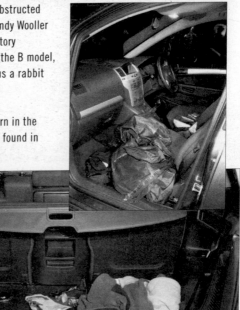

Above and below: Images from the Met CCTV camera near the Honor Oak ATM of the man we were hunting – tantalising, almost taunting, glimpses, leaving us so close but not close enough.

03:51:23 · 13/08/09

05:44:47 · 18/10/09

Delroy Grant, the Night Stalker, after we finally charged him in 2009.

All photos © The Mayor's Office for Policing and Crime unless otherwise stated